The Nature of Children
(and how to deal with it)

Lilly Maytree

LIGHTSMITH PUBLISHERS
Thorne Bay, Alaska

Copyright © 2021 Lilly Maytree
All rights reserved.

978-1-944798-30-7

No part of this book may be reproduced or transmitted in any form or by any means electronic or mechanical, including photocopying, recording, or by any information storage and retrieval system, without the written permission of the publisher.

Published in the United States by
Lightsmith Publishers
P.O. Box 19293
Thorne Bay, Alaska 99919

Website: www.LightsmithPublishers.com
For information contact: info@LightsmithPublishers.com

Lightsmith Publishers is an imprint of the Wilderness School Institute, a non-profit educational organization that offers outdoor youth activities in wilderness settings, including training in wilderness skills and nature studies, as well as the publication of curriculum on related subjects, through the Wilderness School Press, and their children's imprint Summers Island Press.

The Nature Of Children / Paperback Edition

To those who love their children so much more than they understand them...this book is for you.

The Nature of Children (and How to Deal with It) is a book that covers a wide range of issues people might have with their children. It is practical, sometimes humorous, and quite accurate. I found many statements that I would have made myself. One of my favorite quotes in the book is "Life is full of unspoken principles that nobody talks about but everybody learns." This book will help you make sure that the principles you are teaching your child will be ones you want to teach.

Becky Brown, LMFT, Therapist, International Conference Speaker

CONTENTS

INTRODUCTION

Part One: Behavior in Human Nature

General Behaviors
1. Changing Channels
2. The Sibling Wars
3. Alien Babies
4. Raising Cain
5. Choking Hazard
6. Strictly Confidential

Behavior Management
7. Out of Habit
8. Making Your Point
9. Safeguards
10. Family Law
11. Let the House Rule

Part Two: Changing Behavior

The Structure
12. The Great Controversy
13. Personality Plus
14. Choice Cuts
15. The Winner's Circle

The Program
16. Phase One
17. Phase Two
18. Phase Three

Part Three: Training Up

Raising the Standard
      19. In Training
      20. Living with an Attitude
      21. Making Problems
      22. Common Ground
      23. The Meaning of Things

The Pursuit of Excellence
      24. A Matter of Taste
      25. Doing What's Best
      26. Doing Things on Purpose
      27. About Time
      28. The Search for Together

Part Four: Secrets

For Home
      29. Three Secrets
      30. Just Pretend
      31. Back to School Blues
      32. Bored with it All
      33. Undercover Summers
      34. Going to Extremes

Forever
      35. Touching Bases
      36. Bad Influences
      37. Changing Times
      38. Owning Your Own Home-life
      39. Believe it or Not

Part Five: Helps

40. Point Game for Younger Children
41. Point Chart for Older Children
42. Behavior Contract for Teens

About Lilly Maytree

Other Books By Lilly

About Lightsmith Publishers

"A person's a person, no matter how small..."
Dr. Seus

INTRODUCTION

Today, many of the problems that occur between parents and children are situational. If homework is a chore and bedtimes are worse, chances are, you're a working parent with more than your share of responsibilities for maintaining order in your home. With the high costs of living, rising divorce rates, and multiple marriages becoming the norm, traditional families (with a "stay-at-home" mom and a working dad) are slipping farther and farther away from what is typical in modern lifestyles.

Along with the hustle of today's working parents and hectic schedules, many families are finding that their together time is spent mostly in maintaining order: in the house, at the meals, and especially within those parent/child relationships. Why does a great portion of our communications with children seem to be embroiled with debates over daily chores, bedtime battles, and constant references to boredom at having absolutely "nothing to do?" The answers to these dilemmas lie not in the tearing apart of each particular situation, but within human nature itself. Unlock the secrets of human nature and

> *Unlock the secrets of human nature and you can successfully deal with any child, no matter what age they are.*

you can successfully deal with any child, no matter what age they are.

With a few basic rules that are amazingly simple to apply, you can start seeing results today, and tomorrow, and any other time you would like to "turn the key." And before you say, "But you don't know my kids!" you can be assured that—unless you have given birth to alligators instead of children—these things will work for you. That's because it is the nature of every human to act like a human in any given situation. That is, unless the demands of human nature have been so consistently denied that a human's only recourse is to act like an animal. Which only happens in rare cases, at which point, you would probably be avidly consulting the yellow pages for exorcists instead of just reading up about things.

The truth is, if human nature is the strongest influence on human behavior: working with it instead of against it should produce the best results. And it does. Because even though you can't change human nature, you do possess the power to train up your children to be wonderful human beings by using that very force to your own advantage. Which is perfectly legal, since the laws of human nature are so far above society's laws, they are freely welcomed in every country and culture on earth. For as far back as anyone can remember.

Take Herbert Spencer, for instance. He was excited about this same subject way back during the late eighteen-hundreds, when—as a famous educator in England—he proclaimed, *"Here are the indisputable facts: that the development of children in mind and body follows certain laws...Judge, then, whether all who may one day be parents should not strive with some anxiety to learn what these laws are."*

You might be wondering at this point if you could even find the necessary time it would take to read through such a list, if there happened to be one. After all, time is premium in today's society. Which is why it might cause something of a disturbance to discover that most of what is wrong in today's families can be fixed by spending more time together. Period. So, how do you do that when you've already reached your limits as it is? The secret is changing the time you are already spending with your children, into more worthwhile times.

For example, even though it is human nature for parents and children to want to be together, today's parents are spending less and less time with their children. It started off years ago, when moms left for the working world. And also for reasons which hardly sound threatening at all. Such as, there is simply more for parents and children to do *separately* these days. Sports, entertainment, and social activities for respective age groups are most of what keep people busy outside the family circle. Add to this the advent of microwave cooking, and family members don't even have to keep the same mealtimes when they are all on different schedules.

At the same time, many of the problems encountered in our modern lifestyles can be linked back to one major oversight... nobody is *watching* the children anymore. Not because we don't care. It just isn't entirely necessary. That's because—for the most part—we have traded this old-fashioned pastime for providing something to watch, or be occupied with, themselves. Which frees up busy parents and daycare workers to the point that only "half an eye" is needed to keep things running smoothly. As children grow older, one doesn't even need that.

But the new method has long-term side effects.

Over a period of time, it has a tendency to "desensitize" both the parent and the child. After a while it becomes more difficult to pick up on each other's personality and habits enough to be able to detect—much less predict—what they are really up to. Which doesn't matter too much as long as everyone is behaving. It's when they aren't that misunderstandings begin to flare up at alarming rates. These things also have a tendency to go hand-in-hand with a lack of communication. Angry outbursts, hurt feelings, and misbehavior patterns that seem to hang on no matter what is tried, are often the result of these lack of sensitivities to each other.

All in all, it seems our modern times and inventions have managed to draw a curtain over human nature, hiding the fact that most of our problems stem from our efforts to sever the human from the nature. Exactly how this happened is nobody's fault, as it was never put to a general vote. Still, all of us are left to grapple individually with results in the best way we can. Which, as with any mix-up, can be unraveled the fastest when we go back to the basics. There are many ways to accomplish this. But one of the most important things to take into consideration while making any changes is that you do not waste what precious little time you do spend with your children, sparring about things you cannot change.

Children do not want to hear about the way things are; they want to hear about the way things are with you and them. Right now. Children live in the here and now. Yet, as parents, we tend to spend a lot of time trying to explain the high cost of living to eight-year-olds, or our lack of energy for games to preschoolers whose idea of what you actually even DO at work has never entered their minds.

Which is a waste of time.

If we are going to stick to basics we should start off by looking a little closer at Nature itself. Nature is consistent. You will never see a butterfly hatching out of a spider's egg. You will never see a rainbow on a clear, sunny day. A baby bird will push siblings out of the nest to assure its own survival; while a human will not only give up food for a sibling, but in some cases, sacrifice life itself to protect that family member. Nature is fascinating and amusing beyond measure, with multi-layered wisdoms to be discovered there. The order of which, as two of the foremost authorities on the subject (1) once so aptly put it, *"is the largest of all certainties."* Not the least of which is the fact that there is a vital connection between humans and Nature that produces wonderful results whenever we come into contact with it. But one does not *have* to have this in order to survive. Yet, it holds secrets that can make everyday life more meaningful, simply because that's where we originally came from.

In looking at Nature, we find that *consistency is the key to stability.* Nature successfully hosts an innumerable variety of lifestyles, and it manages this through a superb use of balance and consistency. All the creatures of Nature stay in balance within their own space, no matter what Forces of Nature come against them. One never sees a zebra deciding to birth a lion the next season, simply because the lions fared better in the dry season last year. And if we as humans look at our own nature and consider our homes as our hub of existence, then much strength and

> **Consistency is the key to stability.**

confidence for daily life can be gained by bringing a few things back into balance that we have lost sight of there. Which is not to neglect the very nature of our children.

Following is a short list describing the basics of human nature. If you were to close this book afterward and never read further, you could deposit these few items in the bank of your home-life and they will start paying dividends. In fact, the entire book is laid out that way, should you be so inclined (or so pressed for time) that you would rather skip all the explanations and just implement the lists at the end of each chapter. There is even a "quick key" in the back, should you find yourself in a crisis situation that you would like to have help on, right now. After all, the foremost goal for this book is that it would function as a tool—used often—to help today's families maintain themselves on the ever-changing roads of our world.

Here's hoping it will.

Basic Truths of Human Nature:

All humans (even those who have not yet attained the use of language) **WANT TO BE ACKNOWLEDGED**. That means noticed when they come into a room, looked in the eye when they are spoken to, and responded to when they do or say something to others.

All humans respond to praise. **SAY SOMETHING NICE ABOUT THEM** and you have their attention. Instantly.

If you **LISTEN WITH RESPECT** to them, they will

listen with respect to you.

If you **CONSISTENTLY PREDICT HOW WONDERFUL THEY ARE**, they will do everything within their power to rise to your opinion of them.

Contrary to popular opinion, the more **LOVE AND ATTENTION** you shower on a human, the stronger and more independent they will become.

Throughout the following chapters, we will take an in-depth look at each of these principles, and give practical suggestions on how to implement them into real, everyday life. Will it be worth the effort? You bet. Because in spite of the many terrible things people have been saying about it, lately, the human race is still the best thing in the world to be born into. And its children are worth everything we've got.

---

(1)   Sir J.Arthur Thomson and Patrick Gedds, from *Life: Outlines of General Biology*

Part One:

Behavior in Human Nature

General Behaviors

1. Changing Channels
2. The Sibling Wars
3. Alien Babies
4. Raising Cain
5. Choking Hazard
6. Strictly Confidential

Behavior Management

7. Out of Habit
8. Making Your Point
9. Safeguards
10. Family Law
11. Let the House Rule

General Behaviors

1

Changing Channels

The River of Life is wide and swift and success is most often measured by merely making it to the end without piling up on the rocks or drowning along the way. There are many methods of travel. Some simply jump in fully clothed and let the currents carry them however and wherever they will, and others build amazing watercraft to help them along. Still others band together and travel in floating societies, each member specializing in something the others cannot do. These societies have become quite sophisticated. Now, after millennia of advancing humanity, it is possible to make it all the way down without knowing how to swim. Some have even finished without ever actually getting wet. And along the way we have built ourselves up philosophies that tell us it isn't really necessary, anymore.

Everything is taken care of. No worries. If something goes wrong, we're covered, because the insurance people are doing their jobs and they can handle it. That's what we pay them for. Which makes for a nice smooth journey, except for one thing… our children keep jumping over the side. They do not realize the danger of being up so high and are forever fascinated with the water. We call these the "rebellious years" and comfort ourselves with the knowledge that nearly everyone goes through them. Nevertheless, they can give us some of the most heart-wrenching experiences of our lives.

Whether you are the parent or the child.

It is in our nature to want to experience things for ourselves. To accomplish something "on our own", to divide the waters from the waters, and to ultimately see what lies at the end of the River. We don't talk about what lies at the end of the River (even though everone ends up there) because—in our elaborate societies—it simply isn't in good taste. And we spend a lot of time trying to teach our children how to get along in the societies rather than how to get down the River. Figuring out the River is rather old-fashioned, considering the boat is already headed there. So, why all the turmoil?

Because for everything the societies take out of you, the River gives back. Children know this because they spend a lot of time looking. And feeling. For every impression they manage to vocalize they are feeling nine more, and trying to make sense out of them all. It has been said that the human brain absorbs more fully and works faster in childhood than any other time in life. And if that is so, it is prime time for "swimming lessons." The thing about swimming is—outside of a few pointers—it is learned best by doing. Children learn who they are and what they are good at by trying things out for themselves. As soon as they have mastered the home environment, they are ready to explore. They need to explore. Not too far, at first, but they will always be pressing to go farther.

The clash comes because this is a time in the societies when it's a real hassle to get down to the River anymore. We're too busy fulfilling our obligations to the boat, which if we don't keep up, could very well cause us to lose our ticket. Something that is unacceptable. The societies have helped us out a bit in this struggle by providing pastimes for children that fit in with the routine of daily living. Except these only suppress the latent impulses of human nature temporarily, storing up ammunition for the coming rebellious years. That's because the pastimes are lavishly embellished with stories about... the River.

So, what can we do about all this?

Let's take a better look at the River. There's a reason why it's so appealing to humans: it fulfills their need for adventure, their need to excel, and their need to "touch bases" with a little bit of the nature that courses so strongly through every one of us. ***Adventure*** and ***Excellence***. Everyone dreams about these two things. They are the ultimate goal of every human being, no matter how they choose to achieve it. And—once, again —it is a force so strong that it would be better for us as parents (and children) to work with, instead of against.

Maybe let them fish where they've never fished or explore where they've never explored. Maybe even encourage them in this quest for themselves that they are driven to embark on from their very earliest days. The River of Life is full of many channels—let them experience what it's like to change in midstream once in a while. They won't be successful at everything. In fact, they can't be. But something happens in the mere trying that makes them a stronger, more confident individual. And one day they will happen upon something that will turn them into the very person they were meant to be.

Of course, we're not advocating that you pull out all the stops and give your eleven-year-old the keys to the family car if he asks for them, although that's exactly what Charles Lindbergh was doing at that age, and look what an amazing person he turned out to be. Of course, we've acquired a few too many vehicles on the roads since his day and had to come up with an elaborate set of rules and driver's licenses to keep the chaos at bay. The point here is, at that age the young Lindbergh was not only capable of driving the family car, he became so good at it he was designated the official driver on some of his father's political campaigns. He even went so far as to be responsible for the care and maintenance of the vehicle. He kept detailed records of repairs and fuel consumption, laying a foundation that would serve him later in life and allow him to go where no one else had gone and do what no one else had done. And because of these experiences—one on top of the other—he was ultimately able to change the course of the entire Pacific Campaign during World War II, by showing other pilots how to coax more miles out of the airplane engine than anyone had ever believed possible.

Childhood experiences are important.

They make up the foundations of a person's life, and from it spring hopes, dreams, and—more importantly—values that last through a whole lifetime. All the way down the River. But compared to a lifetime, childhood is relatively short. Today, more than any other time in history, much of what has become "on hand" for children to do, is deceptively passive. Interactive is not the same as active, and sooner or later a person will do what he thinks. Because that's Life and that's what living is all about. So, then it becomes very important how that thinking process is developed. In the same way that the law of gravity is no respecter of persons and "what goes up must come down," the human brain is a processor, and "what goes in must eventually come out."

Be careful what you allow into that wonderful little brain you—as a parent—have been entrusted with. It's the only time in life you will have the sole power to decide what does or doesn't go into it. It's the only time in your life when you will be able to declare what is or isn't worthwhile and have those values carry on beyond your own lifetime. It isn't so much a question of good or bad. Most people desire good things for themselves and their children, and most people are good people. The danger lies in wasting the fertile ground of childhood with pastimes and experiences that simply aren't worthwhile. And because it is the nature of children to amuse themselves with whatever is at hand... make sure you surround them with something of value.

> *"Do you love life? Then do not squander time, for that is the stuff life is made of."*
> Benjamin Franklin

Benjamin Franklin once said, *"Do you love life? Then do not squander time, for that is the stuff life is made of."* As far as we've come in "the societies" over the years, we human beings still only have the same allotment of time doled out to us. Twenty-four hours in every day. Rich or poor, good or bad, no more and no less for everybody. And the truth is, in order for you to help your children have more worthwhile experiences, you might have to do a little "channel changing" yourself, in order to provide opportunities for them.

It takes energy to change channels. A channel is a river of current that will carry you along quite nicely without much effort. But try to get out of it, and you will find some pretty intense resistance is involved. You have to go against the current to get out into another channel, then that one proceeds to sweep you along wherever it's headed. So, what's the point? The point is, each time you accomplish a channel change you get stronger. And the more times you do it, you actually find yourself looking forward to the exertion and the refreshing change of perspective that comes from seeing and experiencing something different. Like working out at a gym: it's hard to go but you feel so much better after you do. Do it enough and you become dedicated to working out, simply because you get "hooked" on feeling good. Pretty soon it becomes a channel, and not difficult to stay in at all. The secret to helping your children experience this is to make sure that the channels available to them are worthwhile ones.

Here are some tips to "get your feet wet" with channel changing:

GET IN THE WATER WITH THEM. Children are like everyone else, it's just as hard for them to change channels when the one they're watching has their full attention at the moment. But if you are going to do it, too… well, then that beats a spectator sport any day.

BE ENCOURAGING. Nobody's born a profes-sional and even Charles Lindbergh spent a lot of time fixing flats and running into ditches during his early years. Sometimes a "Let's see if we can fix that," or "Let's try that again," is all it takes to develop persistence in learning something new.

DON'T CRITICIZE FAILURES. People who have accomplished the most in life have also experienced the most failures: they seem to go hand in hand. But there is something to be learned in every experience and it is commendable just to see people try. Always remember that a critical remark at an inopportune moment could be taken personally and cause a child to be reluctant at trying new things in the future, no matter how appealing it looks.

DON'T LET YOUR OWN FEARS LIMIT THEM. Don't steer Sarah away from having a bug collection simply because you can't stand "creepy crawlies." She might be the next Madame Curie.

PAY SOME RESPECT. Give your child your full interest when they are sharing something with you. Replace some of those worn out phrases like "That's nice, hon," or "Cool," with things like "I'm not surprised, you've always been good at figuring things out." Or, "Do you have any plans on how you're going to do that?" And then listen.

HELP THEM OUT WITH AN IDEA now and then. Children get in ruts, too, and sometimes they just can't think of anything to do. That's the time to put your own thinking cap on and come up with an activity or project that you know they would enjoy, even if it takes a little extra time and effort on your part.

Changing channels and experiencing new things can add new dimensions to not only your children's lives, but yours too. You might find yourself seeing things through the eyes of a child, again, and that's a rare and wonderful experience in these hectic times. What's more, you might discover that you're living with one of the most fascinating individuals of our day, right there in your own home. So, don't let hours or days go by without spending "prime time" with your children instead of pastimes, because it all goes by very quickly. And—above all—never be afraid of your child's insatiable pursuit of **Adventure** and **Excellence**...

They make wonderful companions.

The Sibling Wars

Years ago, the phrase "sibling rivalry" was coined by some eminent psychologist and a whole new generation of rebels was born. A rally cry for independence went up and forces began marshaling for a war on the traditional behaviors of children. It was a war that was fought here at home. It was long and drawn out and went on for many years, rolling in and over homes, leaving in its wake a wide path of the destruction of early American values.

There was chaos in the aftermath and some minor pockets of protest went up. It was even rumored in a few circles that whispers of forbears long dead could be heard among the rubble. But it was a new age. The world was different now, and demanded a difference in society. A new generation came along that believed everything told to them… and they agreed. It was said that the most important thing about raising children was to let them "find themselves." That as parents, we must guide but never force them to our own set of values because this would somehow thwart the strengths they would need later in this new, more modern world.

To tell a child "no" was looked down upon. To let them figure things out for themselves as opposed to telling them what to do was the preferred method of teaching children how to get along in an ever-changing world. Something called "situation ethics" was born. It was recognized that older children sometimes felt resentful toward younger siblings, and this was quickly reinforced as being acceptable. In fact, expressing dislike for a sibling was also acceptable, because feelings were not only true but reality to whoever was experiencing them, and therefore should be expressed. Never, under any circumstances, should a parent put a child's feelings down as being right or wrong. Because whatever a child was feeling, it was real for them.

Although this theory has an interesting premise, the fact remains that—since the widespread acceptance of its philosophy—the atmosphere in our schools and our families has been on a steady decline. In a well-known statistical study of the nineteen-fifties, it was said that the types of infractions school children were being corrected for then was gum-chewing, talking in class, and failure to complete assignments. In the nineties, children of the same age and station were getting in trouble for assault, bringing firearms to school, and rape.

These days we have bullying, hate crimes, and even murder. Not to mention the rising number of suicides that has spread even to elementary grades. Homes are now rife with bickering and sibling quarrels. Because of these things, many of our children grow up feeling hatred and resentment for brothers, sisters—and sometimes even parents—for the way things are. What happened?

The Nature Of Children

A look back into the society of our near past shows that we dropped a few things. Simple but vital things. They can be seen the clearest in well-worn phrases that can still be remembered by some of our older members of society. Phrases that spread beyond social station or religious beliefs. They were common sense for the common good handed down by the common people. Here are a few of them:

* If you can't say something nice, don't say anything at all.
* Wrong is wrong, even if it helps you.
* Don't call names.
* Respect your elders.
* The older is responsible for the younger.
* Treat others the way you would like to be treated by them.
* Do your duty.

These are high ideals when looking at them through today's many shades of enlightenment. But in yesterday's society, they were the bottom line. So, what do they have to do with the problems of today? What help are they for working parents, single parents, or part-time parents who are just trying to hone out some little corner for themselves and their children that they can cling to and proclaim as family life? What is your family life truly like? Is your home a haven you can't wait to return to at the end of each day? Do your children think you are the most wonderful person since "Peter Pan" and are they the people you most like to spend your time with?

Yet, there are a few things that haven't changed as the years have gone by and the centuries have turned. Children still come into the world the same way, and they grow the same way. They learn the same way. Ninety percent of today's parents still love their children more than anything else and want what is best for them. They want them to succeed. They want them to attain higher and better things than they themselves did. For the most part, children and parents love each other. Parents are certainly spending more on their children today than at any other time known to man. So, what's the difference?

> *If you are consistent with the consequences of unacceptable behaviours, they will diminish.*

The difference is, we have stopped correcting our children for their attitudes.

Get the attitudes right and the behavior will follow.

Tired of being a referee and judge for the constant competitions and disagreements between your children? Then decide not to have any more fighting in your house. Fighting gets both parties in trouble. Focus on respect for the family and each other instead of disagreements. Does this mean no one can ever have an opposite opinion, or that you will never have another brawl break out after you make this rule?

Not hardly. But if you are consistent with the consequences of such behaviors, they will diminish. And after a while they will disappear altogether, because you have drawn the line. You have pulled rank and used your authority as a parent by setting down the rules, and—no matter what society's trends from one generation to another are—it is human nature to not only submit to authority but to seek it out. If you as a parent do not exert authority over your children, they will search for it somewhere else. That's human nature.

Here are a few simple rules that deal with attitudes that can change the atmosphere in your home from now on:

NO FIGHTING OR ARGUING ALLOWED. If there is a disagreement, it must be dealt with through proper channels, such as the family conference, or by working out a compromise without the use of hitting, yelling, or insults. A fight or an argument must always lead to consequences for both parties APART from the disagreement, itself, which should be handled separately.

NO NAME CALLING. Children need to be encouraged to look for the good in each other, and should follow up each infraction of this rule by saying three nice things to or about whoever they insulted.

NO TEASING. This seemingly harmless game almost always leads to arguments or hurt feelings. The best proof of this is to ask any instigator if he or she would like the same treatment... the answer is almost always, "no." There are better ways to spend time.

SHOW RESPECT TO PARENTS AND OTHER ADULTS. This means you look at them when they are talking to you, do not use an insulting or disrespectful tone when answering, and never walk away or stomp out of the room before they are finished talking to you. Always answer when you are spoken to. Politely.

BE KIND TO EACH OTHER. If you can't play fair and friendly... don't play.

BE HELPFUL. Don't wait to be asked. If you see someone needs help or something needs to be done, pitch in.

USE COMMON COURTESIES. Say hello and goodbye, good morning and goodnight, excuse yourself if you've been rude, and give out a few hugs every day. If you hurt someone's feelings, apologize.

DO NOT RAISE YOUR VOICE. If you cannot express yourself without yelling, you need to go "cool off" for a while. Yelling starts more arguments than it stops and it is disrespectful to others.

If our homes are not havens, it is simply because—in our modern-day hectic worlds—we ourselves have neglected to make them such. Somewhere, our priorities have tumbled. Here in America, we do not have a "neighborhood patrol" to check up on families that don't have their houses under control. It isn't against the law to have our priorities mixed up. It just isn't very beneficial. Sometimes, it can even be the one thing that keeps you from reaching your goals and being truly successful in life. And it can definitely hinder your children.

In this generation, there are more choices and opportunities available to the individual than any other time in recorded history. But at the same time, there are less "absolutes" to build on. The truth is, no matter how much we build up for ourselves as individuals, we still are a part of—and have to interact with—the whole of humanity. And until some new scientific discovery comes up with a way to utilize that untapped ninety-seven percent of the human brain, we will have to continue to go farther by adding on to what others have built before us. If you look close enough, you will find that the most successful people do not cut off the past for the mere fact that it is outdated, but take with them into the future what has already been proven to succeed.

Times change, people don't.

The most startling discovery of all life might very well be to find out that the "life cycle" actually does run in a circle. There's a plan and a pattern to it. What's happening to us now has happened before, and it doesn't take much of a glimpse into the past to realize there's nothing new under the sun. The greatest advantage we have in this day and age is that we have more freedom to decide what we are going to do with our lives. Freedom is a wonderful thing, and no one—in this country, at least—is going to tell you how or what you should do with the freedom that was handed down to you by others. Part of that freedom is to make your own choices.

So, if while you find yourself weighing the pros and the cons, the good and the bad of things, you come across something that has obviously worked and is working for others... make a change. Take a stand for what you believe in, and then be strong in your proclamation of it. You'll find yourself feeling stronger. And strength—no matter what you believe in—is always respected by others. What's more, you'll find a new more comfortable order in your ranks as your own little family unit "falls into line" behind you. And they will. Because everyone is looking for someone to follow... especially children.

That's human nature.

3

Alien Babies

Many parents of toddlers will agree that there are times when they could swear their children must have come from other planets. It is a time filled with perplexities. It is a time when the things you know outside of your relationship with your child, make little or no difference on most of the issues.

That's because—at this point—your child's relationship with you is their whole world and they are not yet equipped to recognize anything of much importance outside of it. Even their likes and dislikes are based primarily on what your preferences are.

It's a time when whatever emotion you have is the very "button" that turns the same emotion on for them. This little phenomenon is easy to prove: laugh and your toddler will laugh; cry and they will cry; exhibit nervousness and stress and baby will be fretful, too. When you couple this with the fact that—at this age—a child is incapable

> *Your child's relationship with you is their whole world...*

of "putting on airs" and has absolutely no regard for time and place... you are left with the potential for some real "million dollar experiences" in parenthood. (Those are the kind you wouldn't trade for a milliion dollars but wouldn't pay a nickel to go through, again.)

Embarrassments are common, especially in public places. Like the mother who decided to take her rambunctious eighteen-month-old on a walk to the store. The day was beautiful outside and the mini-mart was only three blocks away. He needed to "work off some energy" and the condition of her house proved it. They had a wonderful time walking together. She bought a few items while she was there: milk, bread, and eggs. Why? Because a busy mom has to take these opportunities whenever she can get them. But without thinking, she automatically picked up the same sizes she would have chosen from a larger market. And she would have caught that mistake before it was made if she hadn't had her mind focused on something else. She was thinking she should have brought the stroller.

True, the walk had been lovely, and her boy had enough energy to walk to China. But he had no willpower against the numerous low-level rows of colorful treats one is apt to find at this type of establishment. What's more, he suddenly found himself in the deliriously exhilarating situation of not being tied down or into anything. The moment was short-lived. Mom had a lot of experience with these things already, and had the presence of mind not only to finish her business quickly, but to throw in a small treat for enticing baby outside. Which took all of one block to consume.

The surprise came when "out of the clear blue" and for no

apparent reason, her normally predictable boy could not manage another step. Not even one. Whether it was the unexpected exercise or a little too much of that marvelous sunshine they so needed an hour ago, he was suddenly unbearably tired. And he wanted to be carried. So, Mom shifted the groceries and hefted him onto her hip. Where he fit like a piece in a puzzle because she was well used to carrying him. It was the gallon of milk, eighteen eggs, and econo-size loaf of bread she began to have trouble with. A mere half block and she had to set things down for a moment. Could he walk just a little farther, now?

Absolutely not—he couldn't even stand—his legs had somehow turned into rubber. What's more, his juice treat had "gone right through" not only him but his diaper, and she now had a large wet spot at the middle of her shirt. Not that the occupants in the many passing cars were taking notice. At this point, she really didn't care. She just wanted to get home. So, she traded sides with her two burdens and trudged off, again.

At the end of the block, the gallon of milk fell out because her "wet spot" had seeped through the brown paper and the bag had given way. In a lightning quick "save" she managed to keep a grip on the eggs. Baby thought it was hilarious the way the milk jug bounced and rolled into the gutter. It was all so entertaining. And the noises she was making every time something new happened made things even better. But now, Mom had a real problem.

One can manage lugging two heavy things down a road, but not four. Something had to be abandoned— not counting the baby—but which one? As it turned out, it was none. Because when she finally reached for the limits of all her resources, she found she could trudge a few steps ahead with the items, go back for the little limp noodle of a boy, go on past the items again, and so on.

It is amazing how many kinds of situations people can get into, simply because one thing almost always leads to another. Faced with only the end result of an incident—such as walking through the mall with no shirt on—you might say, "Not me, not ever!" However, if baby just threw up every bit of his dinner on your executive cut shirt, you might suddenly think the actual distance back to the car wasn't really that far compared to the alternative. Some people have the same response to vomit as whatever bothered baby in the first place. Which isn't the baby's fault.

Babies do not care whether they throw up onto an executive suit or an old sweatshirt. What's the difference? They were feeling sort of pukey. Things happen when a person feels that way. It's just that the communication process at this age is a little too limited to be able to give much of a warning. Only a very alert parent who recognizes that certain "look" has any chance of avoiding such catastrophes.

Parents spend a lot of time trying to figure out what their toddlers want or need and it is often this "missing link" in communications that leads to the most perplexing incidents. What's more, we have collectively forgotten a lot of what we used to know simply by spending the majority of our time with our children by so many parents having to participate in the working world. A lot of time could be spent in discussing the rapid changes in our society here, and the widespread breakup of extended families that puts grandparents and other wise family members too far away to be of much assistance. But it wouldn't change much in the way we do things today.

However, taking a closer look at the nature of babies will. So, here are a few keys to unlock some of their secrets and give you a glimpse into their little world:

BABIES NEED TO BE HELD. Don't just stand there and watch them cry while you try to figure out what in the world they could need when you've already fed, changed, and played with them. Pick them up and think about it. While you're at it, dole out a few words of comfort and encouragement, whether you can figure out what they're for, or not. This gives an instant sense of security that will help any situation. Sixty percent of the time, it takes care of the problem altogether.

NEVER YELL OR RAISE YOUR VOICE to get a baby to quiet down. It will simply upset or startle them into a worse condition than they were in to begin with. Remember, they are "mirrors" at this age. Talk quiet and soothing to them, first. And if you want to see a smile... smile.

USE CONSTRAINT TO CONTROL BEHAVIOR. Is it a chore to shop with Michael because he runs off every time your back is turned? Save your lecture on the dangers of getting lost for a couple years down the line. Right now, he simply doesn't think in those abstract terms no matter how smart he is. So, don't expect him to. Instead, make it a rule that he must hold hands in the store until he is "big enough" not to need to. This incredible maturity might take place on the very next isle, and if it does, let him give it a try. But don't make the mistake of waiting until he strays to say anything. If he is still at your side after two or three seconds, lavish on the praise. Take his hand again while you tell him how impressed you are, and that you'll just have to let him do it again on the next isle. Of course, on the next isle it's five or six seconds. In this way, you "precondition" him into thinking that self-control is a wonderful thing and something to be sought after. This method might take a little more time to implement in the beginning, but it is guaranteed not to take any time at all in the long run. Michael will be keeping an eye on himself by then and quite proud of it.

BE MINDFUL OF PHYSICAL LIMITS. Humans develop faster in those "baby years" than any other time in life. Their bodies are constantly changing. Because of this, they have little or no reserve for being too cold, too tired, or too hungry. So, don't let them get there. Half the cause of "fussiness" in infants comes from their physical lack of ability to stretch these limits at a time when those physical limits are already stretched to capacity. Endurance is not something you learn, it's something you develop. There will be plenty of room for stretching in a year or two, when the mind begins to have more of an influence than the body.

KEEP A SCHEDULE. That doesn't mean you have to be home at the same time every day for baby's feeding and sleeping. It simply means you should make provision for these things so you can offer them at the same time no matter where you are. Toddlers might not have much endurance at this age, but they are extremely versatile. Most can sleep anywhere with a familiar blanket or playpen, and they can eat or drink in almost any environment no matter where they happen to be at these important times.

CRYING ALWAYS MEANS SOMETHING. Contrary to popular opinion, a baby never cries for nothing. Without language, emotions are the only means of communication that infants have at their disposal. A baby that continues to cry after being fed, changed and whatever else you might deem necessary, might simply want to be held for a while. There's nothing wrong with that. And it should come as no surprise that an infant who communicates solely by emotions, should need to be "recharged" every now and then.

DON'T MAKE "NO" SO NEGATIVE. You do not have to yell or show anger in order to say no to your toddler. Keep your tone normal, and should they choose to continue whatever it is you don't want them to do (such as sticking a bobby pin in a light socket), simply go over and physically remove them from the area. If a tantrum ensues, pick them up until it's over. Letting them do the same thing again, and again while you escalate in temper right along with them, doesn't do either of you any good. And don't change your mind and let them do it some days and not others. Remember: intermittent success is much stronger than intermittent punishment, which is one of the strongest influences on human behavior there is. So, it's better to have this force working for and not against you.

Babies are the finest example of love and perfection there is. The pleasure parents take in them are their greatest gift to the family and they naturally draw family members closer together while they draw each one close to themselves. By nature, they are non-judgmental, easily satisfied, and often overjoyed to see the same familiar faces every morning. So, the next time you're tempted to think your baby lives in a "world all their own," try using some of these keys to get inside. And if you'll look close enough once you get there, you'll find you don't have an "alien baby," after all. Just a normal healthy toddler.

The most important thing to remember about getting through the toddler years is that satisfaction leads to contentment. But there is more to satisfaction than just meeting physical needs. History shows us in the tragedy of war orphans that—without any physical affection or holding—many infants put in large orphanages, died. Our great-grandmothers reinforced this knowledge with the old adage that you can't spoil a child by holding them too much... it actually works the other way around.

And she was right.

4

Raising Cain

Being young in this day and age has its advantages. And disadvantages. While our modern medicine has made the journey through the first five years less hazardous, our dependence on preserved foods and indoor entertainment has hindered the development of healthy bodies. And while we have successfully abolished child labor, young people who should be "getting their feet wet" in the working world feel little need to do so. Nobody likes wet feet.

Similarly, many of the natural impulses of human nature, such as the craving of acceptance and a perpetual striving toward independence, have become more of a burden than a benefit in our new and more complicated societies. We have devised "band-aids" for most of these conditions but—like aspirin—they only provide temporary relief and not a cure. All things considered, it should be no surprise to find the ones that have the most difficulty with these changes are the teens.

The only thing that a teenager lacks in the ability to do

anything an adult can do is experience. Yet, in these days when we have advanced farther, we have – for some reason – severely cut back on what we allow our teens to do. When they reach driving age, we penalize them by charging more for auto insurance. True, it can be argued that more teens get into accidents than adults. But it is also true that more teens do not get into accidents than do. A sliding scale for those that don't do well in the early stages of their driving skills seems much more appropriate than punishing all teens for having reached that particular age. Along the same lines, most businesses (other than the service industry) have stopped raising up new workers by hiring teens as apprentices. We now have specialized schooling for the higher paying jobs, which — ironically — cost more to attend than most young people can afford without outside help.

Thus the "generation gap" between teens and adults has stretched wider than any other time in history. And with good reason.

For the most part, our teenagers of today are extremely frustrated. Their physical, mental, and moral capacities are working at a more furious rate than they ever will, again, in their lifetime and there are little or no outlets for them. So, it's no wonder that many parents are confronted with attitudes of **disrespect**, **disregard**, and **isolation**. These attitudes are so widespread and prevalent that they have now been labeled as "normal" behaviors of the teen years.

Like the "terrible twos" of the toddler years, the rebellion of our teenagers has become something that we, as parents, have simply accepted and gear up for. But isn't there some way around it all? You bet there is. And that is to go back to where we lost our way in the first place and take a closer look at those three terrors that have managed to knock us off course.

Disrespect

Webster's Dictionary defines respect as "esteem, regard, or relating to a particular person or thing." Mutual respect – or esteem – comes from admiration. Respect comes from respect. It is a tangible thing that is passed between individuals as a result of interaction. Parents and children have an advantage bestowed on them by human nature: in the beginning of their relationship they start out by being in absolute awe of each other.

Respect has nothing to do with age or position (although these elements can influence one way or the other as time goes on). That's why a fully mature adult can respect the ultimate perfection of a baby for the sheer wonder of humanity. One isn't normally repulsed by the fact that an infant can't communicate verbally at that point, or participate in securing the family income. On the other hand, to disrespect someone, is to not have any regard for their personal position at all: a result of having broken down the natural impulses toward respect that we are born with.

Disregard

> Life is choices.

Disregard is not the same as disrespect, though disrespect leads to it. To come to the place where one willfully refuses to acknowledge a particular person or circumstance, is an outcome of disagreement. Life is choices. Many times we will have to make a personal decision about which road to take in Life's journey and children begin participating in this process long before they reach an age of maturity. For the most part, their decisions will be based on circumstances and projected outcome. If your children have chosen to disregard your authority in certain areas, then it is their reasoning you must deal with and not their actions.

That isn't to say that actions shouldn't have consequences, but at this point, the actions are merely the outcome. The problem is rooted in the mind and not the body. Open disregard of your rules or authority simply means the bridges of communication have broken down and it's time to go back and make repairs. If left unresolved for too long, the trouble can spread to the heart: which almost never gets settled without serious losses on both sides. And sometimes never get resolved at all.

Isolation

Isolation is the outcome of being repeatedly ignored or looked down upon. It is the defense mechanism of those who have been continually challenged or disagreed with. Left by itself, this response can have a positive effect, in that a normal human being will eventually crave acceptance more than independence, and swing back toward the norm. The trouble with today's malcontents of the teen world is that there are so many of them, they provide their own society of acceptance to get them through these times. Thus, it is often well into adulthood that individuals are still learning lessons in life and relationships that should have been settled in their formative years.

Because of this, there are often already new children on the scene who are put on a disadvantage at an early age due to an environment of warped behaviors that they assume to be normal. This situation can cause even greater problems down the line when human nature begins to clash with society's challenges. For example, the isolation response can cause a child to withdraw from family and friends until the craving for acceptance forces them to return to accepted behavior. With adults, however, isolation can so estrange an individual that their only recourse is to revert to retaliation against society instead of compliance with it. An estranged adult is far more volatile than an estranged child.

Contrary to popular opinion, disrespect, disregard, and isolation, are serious matters. Not to deal with them opens the door to problems that cannot only take a lifetime to unravel but cause painful consequences for others in the meantime. So, here is a list of seven things that parents can do today, to prevent teens from having to resort to any of these uncomfortable behaviors tomorrow.

SHOW RESPECT. You do not have to agree with your teenager, or even allow them to repeatedly break rules in your home that you have set down beforehand. But you do have to show them respect as a person. That means treating them with the same courtesies that you would expect your boss at work to treat you. You would not like to be yelled at, put down or called inferior names, or ignored completely when you are expressing your opinions.

BE AGE APPROPRIATE. Don't treat a seventeen-year old like a fourteen-year-old. Responsibility leads to being responsible. If you aren't trusting your older teen with the care and use of family assets such as the car and the house, then the resulting immaturity will not only lead to arguments, but resentments. On both sides.

BE FAIR. Kids these days have few places in which to "hang out" and do things together other than a theater or the local mall. So, unless you want to become one of those parents who "can't understand what came between you and your child," decide on specific times and rules, and let them be a host in their own home on a regular basis. NOTE: in this instance, regular does not mean only once a year on their birthday.

BE SENSITIVE. Just because you don't see an immediate reaction to your approval or disapproval, don't assume there isn't any. Your judgments will always have an effect on your children whether they admit it or not. One need only look back to their own teen years to remember how emotional they are. Or how discouraging a parent can be that pushes too hard or nags too much during those unsettling times.

ALWAYS PROVIDE A WAY BACK. If your teen has made a big mistake of some kind, don't hold it over his head until voting age. Everybody makes mistakes. Help him find a way to make it right, and after he takes that way... let it go.

DON'T BELITTLE STRONG FEELINGS. Don't joke or make fun of genuine emotions, especially in front of others. Even if Jenny loved the boy-next-door, yesterday, and can't stand the sight of him, today, she will come to the right conclusions about the matter on her own.

BE BRAVE. In a very short time, your darlings will be off on their own without having to consult you for anything. So, if they feel a hankering to "try their wings" with a few things, let them. Even the eagles fly beneath their young for a while before letting them venture out into the skies alone.

Raising teenagers in a world where most teenagers are "raising Cain" can be an emotional roller coaster for both parents and teens. But if you remember to face their disrespect with your respect for them; their disregard with your own love and faith in them; and their isolation with an open acceptance of who they are and where they belong in the world, then your teenagers will not go through the rebellion that most kids do, these days.

They won't have to.

Choking Hazard

It is dangerous to be a child in this day and age. A lot of things have changed since you were there, especially the predators. They have to change—those things that prey on the young—because down through history parents have been great at taking care of pretty much anything that threatened the safety and welfare of their children. Like childhood diseases. We hardly give them a thought anymore, except to try to keep up with current inoculations. And as for wild things sneaking into the cave at night to see what they can haul off...

Well, most of us don't live in caves anymore, either. But the rapid advance of our modern lifestyles and conveniences have brought along complacencies that are largely dependent on the false sense of securities we have built up for ourselves. Phrases like, "Kids grow up faster these days—they're tougher," are substantiated by the advent of the Information Age, which makes anything and everything available at the turn of a switch to anyone and everyone. Including children.

But it isn't the children who have changed, only the times. A toddler will put a small mysterious object in the mouth to test what it might be, just as quickly today as one would two thousand years ago. And a teenager will pledge allegiance to a friend—as if they were family— just as quickly as one would back in the middle ages. Times change. People don't. The only difference is, that parents today satisfy themselves with the fact that they have adequately paid someone (preferably professionals) to watch over their toddlers throughout the day while they are at work. Or that their errant teens are only responding (quite naturally) to what is referred to as "the rebellious years." But to think that others can take the place of a parent–no matter how well paid—is a fallacy only our modern times have fallen prey to. That's because there is no eye like the watchful eye of a parent.

> Times change, People don't.

No one knows a child better than a parent, and no one can reach that child better than a parent. Why is that so? Because children are made in the image of their parents. That's the nature of things. Humans come with the incredible power to "create in their own image," and they do. They are continuing to do so every day of the year. For better or for worse. We do it every day of our lives as our children (by nature) copy our own actions and mannerisms.

But the truth is, the changing times are affecting parents as much as their children. We—like the children —tend to believe everything we see in print, or hear on TV. Never in all of history has the individual opinion been so far down on society's "priority list." What does the doctor have to say? What does the school recommend? And what did they say in that latest poll taken by CNN?

The Nature Of Children

Our children are like ourselves. That's why we are so attached to them when they first come along. Add to the fact that one spends nearly every waking hour with them when they first arrive, it's no wonder we know so exactly what "makes them tick." Any mysteries we run into can usually be answered by a spouse who recognizes the off-beat characteristic from his or her side of the family. Inherited traits and tastes perpetuate themselves. But it is interesting to note that most problems faced by today's families are brought on by the subtle process of becoming "de-sensitized" from these natural things. A process that happens almost subconsciously.

While most parents are aware of the choking hazards that threaten toddlers (and take care to prevent those incidents from occurring) not many realize that there are similar hazards that an older child can "choke on" later on, that could have been prevented by the same kind of watchfulness. The standard rule of not letting them take "too much too fast" applies just as well to a teenager as it does for a tot: they're just dabbling in different things.

In the same way, the old rhyme that a "stitch in time will save nine," is true. And whoever came up with the philosophy that "an ounce of prevention is worth a pound of cure," was nearing the pinnacles of wisdom when it comes to avoiding catastrophes. The real secret to avoiding pitfalls in any society —including our own —is still to learn how to recognize warning signs and do something about them before things happen.

Here's a list of things that will help:

FIND OUT SPECIFICALLY WHAT YOUR KIDS ARE DOING. Vague generalities like, "Just playing outside," or "At a friend's house," could include activities such as starting fires or watching R-rated movies. So before you answer with an equally vague, "That's nice, dear," it might be important to find out exactly what they were playing, and whose house they were in.

DON'T ALLOW SECRETS. Unless it's a holiday where presents are exchanged, children should not be keeping secrets from their parents. Nor should they be allowed to keep parents out of their room if they so choose. It's one thing to give a courteous knock on a closed door before entering but any child who knows a parent can and will move freely in and out of their room, will not only be careful of what they keep there, they will also be careful how they behave there.

DON'T LET FEELINGS OVERRIDE YOUR FAMILY'S STANDARD OF CONDUCT. Being tired, or angry, or not feeling well, is no excuse for bad behavior. You can be sympathetic toward these conditions (and even ward off an incident if you see them coming beforehand) but never withhold correction because of them. Nurturing self-control has many more benefits than nurturing selfishness.

WATCH OUT FOR THE SMALL STUFF. Do you detect a hint of disrespect in a response, or a lack of cooperation in trying to get along? Better to deal with these things immediately, because – like weeds – they are much harder to get rid of later on.

MAKE A BIG DEAL OUT OF THE MAJOR STUFF.

Violence, stealing, smoking or experimenting with drugs and pre-marital sex, are extremely serious offenses and they deserve extremely serious consequences. Extending periods of "time out" or "being grounded" is not enough. These behaviors call for a form of restitution and – in some cases – even a complete change of environment and peer involvement. If you don't, society will do it for you sooner or later, and the end results can be much more devastating than it would have been coming from you. Take these matters too lightly, and your children will, too.

PROVIDE ACCEPTABLE OUTLETS FOR ENERGY AND ASPIRATIONS. Many problem behaviors stem from a lack of supervision coupled with boredom. It is better for children to be involved in too much than too little, and a structured activity beats long hours with nothing to do but the "same old things."

BE PHYSICAL. Touch, hug, and play with your children often. These are natural "barometers" for true feelings, and will delight them no matter how old they are. This kind of interaction can also defuse bad attitudes faster than a lecture. Sort of like turning a light on in a dark room.

Today's predators are more subtle than those we find in history. They are poisonous messages smuggled in through mixed media that undermine the values of family living. They are the ability of your children to keep bad company for long periods of time before you realize it and then resent you for taking them away. They are the natural wonders of nature pushed so far back from our modern cities that few children can discover them for themselves, anymore. They are too many things in exchange for a sense of value.

Taken all together over extended periods, these subtle enemies have the power to choke the life out of normal healthy children and leave them weakened in many ways. But they are no match for a normal healthy parent who knows how to handle them and what to watch out for. You do it by making yourself more aware of what you are really giving to your children. And if you should discover a "warning: choking hazard" sign on one of those things...

Don't buy it.

6

Strictly Confidential

Even as there are certain things that should not be discussed on the evening news, there are also personal issues within families that should not be discussed in public. In this day and age when society has successfully broken out of the Victorian Era, no subject is "taboo." But even though a majority of parents seem to pride themselves for "telling it like it is" to their children, a few casualties have occurred in the crossfire. Like *confidence* and a *sense of conscience*. One does not need these two things in order to survive.

It's just that life is a lot better with them than without them.

Confidence is not limited simply to the faith one has in oneself. It is also the faith one builds through experience in the people and things around them. Through the consistent availability of food, clothing and shelter offered by parents, most children go to bed each night without having to worry where they will obtain these things the following day. They do not even have to know the details of how provisions will come, they simply accept the fact that they will be there. They have faith in those things, and there is no fear involved in that area of their lives.

When it comes to relationships, it's a different matter. Will Mom be in a good mood or a bad one this morning? Is she kidding or does she really mean it this time? Is she ignoring me, or just not listening right now? These are questions a child must calculate and figure out every day. The phenomenon here, is if a parent's actions are erratic, it is the child who takes the blame. Why? Because it is the nature of children to trust their parents. And if for some reason a parent proves untrustworthy... the child feels insecure.

Which results in a lack of confidence.

What's more, it is also in the nature of children to emulate their parents. If it is acceptable in your home to tease or "put each other down" as a mode of entertainment, don't be surprised when your child can't tell the difference between your home or friend's house. Or a public place. Take the library, for instance. There are no signs that read "Quiet Please," before you walk in. Yet, it is accepted behavior for people to "lower their voices" when inside. If one does not instruct their children in accepted library behavior, there will be an irate librarian that will do the task for you. This will result either in an embarrassing moment for your child, or the loss of library privileges. A child who enters the library knowing the rules beforehand, does so with confidence. He then goes on to discover the pleasures of the many things that are offered there.

Whoever said, "knowledge is power," was not far wrong. For what we know, we have faith in. It's those unstable "gray areas" that seem to be where all the problems arise. But how does one get rid of them? It is human nature to create standards for oneself, and — for the most part — what is done consistently, will set the standard. High or low, good or bad, does not apply here. A parent that complains, "How can you stand living in such a messy room?" will almost always

> *What we know, we have faith in.*

get a blank or indifferent response from their child, for the simple reason that – up until that moment – it has not been a family priority to take care of it. However, the child's response to this will not be to point out the parent's inconsistency, but to feel a lack of *confidence in themselves...* because they really are quite comfortable with it.

If dishes are done every night after dinner, a child left to himself will do the dishes after dinner. His *conscience* will make him uncomfortable if he does not, simply because it is the family habit. The parent who never insists on help from a child for such chores, will come home under the same circumstances and find the dishes left undone, with no *conscious sense* that they should have been. What's more, arguments and ill feelings are likely to ensue if the parent wants to make an issue out of it. An "unstable home" does not always mean a broken or poverty-ridden one. It simply means that there are no absolutes there. That your home-life might be peaceful one day but volatile the next. That the members of your family might be on the best of terms one moment and at odds with each other the next.

This kind of instability leads to a lack of confidence and conscience in children. The truth is, this is a very common problem and happens even in the "best of circles." Does this mean that the human race is on a decline in these modern times and there isn't much we can do about it?

Not at all, and here are some things that will help:

BE SENSITIVE TO YOUR CHILDREN'S SENSITIVITIES. Never speak about your children to a third party as if they weren't there. If your children are present when you are sharing about them, include them in the conversation. And be careful what you share. Certain things are inappropriate in a group—not because they are right or wrong—but because of the age of the child. All humans have trouble with "irregularity" now and again. But to mention the problem your twelve-year-old daughter is having in front of others would be absolutely mortifying for her.

DON'T ALLOW YOUR CHILDREN TO BELITTLE DIFFERENCES. Does Jerry like blue when Sally likes pink? There is no right or wrong to that. To argue about it makes children insecure about themselves. The old adage *"sticks and stones may break my bones but words can never hurt me,"* is a fallacy. Words can have life-changing effects… especially coming from loved ones.

MEAN WHAT YOU SAY AND SAY WHAT YOU MEAN. Don't make your children have to figure you out all the time, and—most importantly—never lie to them. The natural reaction to lies (especially from loved ones) is betrayal.

MAKE UP A SCHEDULE whether you need one, or not. Knowing what's coming next gives a child a sense of security. Even something like, "We have spaghetti on Tuesday and pizza on Friday," can provide a comfortable haven from a world that is full of far too many choices for young psyches.

MAKE ROOM FOR QUIET. Children should not be busy every moment of the day any more than adults should be. They need time to think and contemplate things and *discover* who they are, as opposed to simply making choices. In this day and age when we are bombarded by so much noise we tend to "tune out" instead of turn off, we have almost forgotten the benefits of peace and quiet. Even ten or fifteen minutes a day can have a wonderful effect... on everyone.

SAY SOMETHING NICE TO EACH OTHER EVERY DAY. If you haven't shared a laugh or a smile or even a scrap of pleasant conversation all day, don't let them go to bed without it. These good things go straight to the heart, and work as a preventive against bad attitudes.

BE YOUR BEST AROUND YOUR CHILDREN and they will knock themselves out trying to be their best around you.

All of these seemingly simple things can protect your family from not only the instability of our times, but the instability of home-life, as well. What goes on in most homes every day is—for the most part—very private. Sometimes things can get way out of hand before anyone on the outside even notices. Because of this, it helps to take an honest look at your family life once in a while and decide if it really measures up to what you would like it to be. If it doesn't, remember that big changes often come about in small ways. You can make a major difference by simply deciding to do a few small things differently. Confidence and a good conscience will follow, not only for your children… but for you, too.

And you can keep it strictly confidential.

Behavior Management

7

Out of Habit

Everyday life is made up of habits. Even people who claim to be non-conformists are habitual. Do you tend to order the same things at a restaurant? Do you watch the same TV programs? Do you find yourself saying the same things over and over to your kids? All human beings are creatures of habit and it is not a sign of weakness to be habitual.

But it is a sign of strength to *choose your habits*.

It only takes two weeks to create (or break) a habit. If that's true, why aren't we all living at the height of our own capabilities? Mostly because habits are like people's houses... we've lived with them so long they tend to feel comfortable. And most habits aren't really harmful to anyone. Except for a few extremely bad ones, which society has a tendency to press in on us, if we continue to exhibit them. But they're also a lot like living room clutter: not really bothering anything, but not helping anything, either. Here's how to judge a habit: is it a help, or a hindrance?

If Johnny is a picky eater because he doesn't like to eat vegetables, that's a hindrance. On the other hand, if he breaks out in hives every time he eats tomatoes, it's a help for him not to do that. Help or hindrance. It's a good idea to take stock of your family's habits once in a while. Why? Because too many hindrances in an already hectic lifestyle can complicate things. For instance, if there's an argument every night about whose turn it is to do dishes; getting into the habit of posting a weekly schedule might be a help. In the same way, if everything that comes out of your children's mouths is either whining or argumentative, then a little "habit forming" in social skills might be in order. Politeness doesn't only work with strangers.

> *Never try to change more than one habit at a time.*

It is much easier to change the habits of children than adults, simply because of their enthusiasm for new things. It's part of their nature. And the secret of changing the habits of children successfully is to make the changing process positive. The way to do this is:

*Never try to change more than one habit at a time.

*Have a *"fair exchange"*: **Never take something away without putting something better in its place**. If you're trying to get Sara to stop picking her nose or sucking her thumb, it's going to take some real incentives to get her to want to – simply because there are some deeply ingrained gratifications at work here. Catch her *not doing it* and lavish on the praise. Notice her trying hard and give her an unexpected reward. Give her something she can earn by going X amount of minutes, hours, or days without doing it until the habit is no longer there (please note that an incentive is *not* a smack every time you catch her doing it… that will only train her to resent you for taking the comfort away). It is also helpful to introduce something acceptable to do with one's hands during this time, like holding a toy with many textures.

* **Set up a routine.** Do it every day, for three weeks, preferably at the same time. Habits are consistent by nature. Trying to make or break one by the "hit and miss" method is an automatic set up for failure. That's because you'll always revert to doing what you do the most.

* **Be encouraging** but try not to nag. Contrary to popular opinion, nagging puts more distance between you and your child's cooperation, not less. Nagging is like an itch: the more you do it, the more you have to.

Habits define character. And if developing good habits is a form of building better character in our children, let's take a closer look at the building process. In its simplest form, the word building means "adding to." Here's an example. In order to construct a building, one adds material from the ground up until a structure, that is suitable to the purpose, rises to completion. Sometimes areas that will receive excessive use (or stress levels) are "reinforced." This process is carried out by adding more material to strengthen what is already there. To remove support in those vital areas, would only serve to weaken the structure and possibly even hinder the final usefulness of it.

It's the same way with building character.

One reinforces character by seeking out strong points and "adding strength to strength." To tear someone down (by negative criticism, insults, name-calling, or punishment) never adds to the "building process." It only hinders it. So, if you --

as a parent -- are in the habit of resorting to any of these methods to change the way your children do things and are not having much success, chances are the children aren't the only problem.

So, how do we go about adding "strength to strength" instead? By using the strongest tool a parent has at their disposal. It's called modeling. If it is true that your child will walk like you walk, talk like you talk, eat like you eat—simply from living with you—then it is also true that they will mirror your habits. Good and bad.

Would you like your teenaged daughter to show you a little more respect around the house? Try giving her a pleasant acknowledgement when she enters the room, or when you pass in a hallway. Give her *your* full attention when she has something to say (no matter how busy you are), and dole out about three times ***more complements*** than criticisms during a day. Stop telling and start showing... it's the fastest teaching method known to man. It's the difference between being the boss and being bossy.

In the same way that "we are what we eat," our children are what we are. Plain and simple. That's why taking stock now and then of family habits strengthens the whole family. Following is a list of a few habits that will make a difference in your home no matter what lifestyle you follow.

> **DONATE ONE HOUR OF TV TIME A WEEK FOR A FAMILY ACTIVITY** (a board game, reading out loud, an outside activity, or even a group treat with small talk). Make sure this is prearranged, so no one's favorite show is left out. With so much "down time" on TV these days when nothing is worth watching, a single hour is not difficult to come up with.

HAVE A FAMILY MEAL ONCE A WEEK, where the whole family sits around the table at the same time and eats the same things.

GO TO THE LIBRARY AS A FAMILY, every week, for one hour, for one month.

TAKE TURNS AMONG FAMILY MEMBERS TO CHOOSE A TOPIC FOR DISCUSSION AT DINNER (at the family dinner if you are only together once a week). One topic per meal. If children are younger, it helps to pre-announce the topic to parents before time, so they can help "jump start" conversations that stall too soon.

ASSIGN THE HOUSEKEEPING CHORES of one room (other than bedrooms) to family members for one week on a rotating basis.

DO AT LEAST ONE THING FOR SOMEONE ELSE EVERY DAY.

READ FOR FIFTEEN MINUTES AT BEDTIME EVERY NIGHT.

Remember, work on building only one habit at a time. Too much change at once can be hard to cope with in a busy family, and success levels drop when there are too many things competing with each other. Doing something every day for three weeks creates a habit, and the things mentioned here are only a few suggestions to help you get started. But when you see how beneficial even these small things can be, you'll enjoy making a "wish list" of the way you'd like your family to be all the time. What's more, you'll know the secret of how ***you can get there***.

You get there out of habit.

8

Making Your Point

Many of the problems that confront today's families stem from a lack of communication. Not the ordinary kind. Most families are well equipped with a system of gestures, words and phrases that convey the basic fundamentals of daily living. Everyone knows what to expect. But there are times when our communication skills need to go a little farther past basic.

"She won't clean her room. She'd rather fool around in there for three hours than just get it over with. And when she finally does make an effort...it's not even half right." What exactly do you mean when you say clean? Pick up the toys? Make the bed? Put dirty clothes in the hamper? Are you really going to be picky about the dried up bit of juice that spilled from yesterday's snack when you weren't that picky last time? And why should the wastebasket be emptied when it's only half-full?

Cleaning could mean anything from shoving toys and clothes into a single heap in the closet and making the bed, to vacuuming and washing the walls. Depending on what day it is and what sort of mood *you* are in. Children know these things.

And subconsciously, they are as fascinated or perplexed with how you think as you are with them. "She left that wet bath towel right in the middle of the bed again—what was she thinking?" Definitely not about wet towels.

Maybe you have demonstrated ten times to Joey how to pull the sheet up first and then the blankets – so why shouldn't you be a little exasperated when you discover that telltale lump at the foot of the bed after he has already run out to play? Do you think maybe your teenager wasn't listening when you explained how to light the barbecue and then watched him proceed to produce a ten-foot burst of flame that nearly ignited the covered patio? How difficult could it be? Pile up the charcoal, squirt on the starter, light and toss the match. But what if it doesn't "catch on right" and he thinks maybe there isn't enough starter? If your previous fire safety courses only covered the "stop, drop and roll" situations, chances are, the mistake might have been... on your end.

Parents are teachers (whether they choose to be, or not) and one doesn't travel far along the road of parenthood without bumping into some dilemmas over the best way to make a point. There are many methods for teaching. But the first and foremost goal in any subject for any age is to make your point. Start the ignition, and make sure there is a connection before you go "troubleshooting" down the lines. Many of the common problems between parents and children exist because that initial "connection" was never engaged in the first place.

Life is full of unspoken principles that nobody talks about but everybody learns. We file these things quickly away into our subconscious in order to make room for the current, more difficult tasks. From that point on, they rarely have to pass through the brain again before being converted into action. Parents almost always forget this. They seem to think their children should have a ready store of this "common sense" available to them, even though they have physically not had enough time to collect it all, yet.

This is one place where the animals have us beat (making the theory of evolution a bit shady, here) because many of them are born with an imprint of this kind of knowledge fully intact A baby turtle that emerges from the egg makes a mad dash for the sea. It does not need a parent standing on the beach shouting, "Run, kids, run! One foot in front of the other!" Similarly, you can put a homing pigeon in a box and release it miles away in unfamiliar territory and it will still find home. This is instinct. And we humans don't come with any of that stuff. We might be born with a fully developed, perfect set of equipment (heart, lungs, eyes, etc.) but it's all potential. What we do with that equipment is mostly developmental. And—as humans —much of our development is dependent on outside influences.

> *Life is full of unspoken principles that nobody talks about but everybody learns.*

At the same time, that wonderful phenomena we call learning can take place from the most basic, "Watch me, kid, you might learn something," to that elaborate system of breaking and remaking of character set down by our military. Or anything in between. An interesting point here is that some of the most complicated systems tend to produce the quickest results. At first glance, it might seem odd that our military programs—with a goal to train up soldiers for the defense of our country—begin with lessons in how to eat, how to dress, how to walk and how to talk. It's because they are "making a connection." It is a proven fact that everyone who enters the military is in the habit of eating, dressing, walking and talking. By starting here, virtually no one is left out. After that, there are detailed instructions for every step along the way, and nothing is left to the imagination. In fact, there is very little time left in a day to imagine anything at all.

As parents, we have a lot longer than four years to accomplish our goals but many of the same principles apply. Which could also be deceiving because we tend to spend half of our time thinking we have plenty of time to get the job done, and the other half wondering where it all went so fast. Many of us find ourselves in later life, looking into the eyes of fully-grown adults where our children used to be, and realize we only covered half of what we meant to over the years. Teachers sometimes feel the same emotions in a mere nine months. But the teaching profession has developed a few sure-fire secrets they can depend on to help them out. They do wonders "out of school," too. So, here they are:

> **BREAK IT DOWN.** Take big tasks (like cleaning a room) and break them down into smaller ones. For example, make the bed, pick up the toys, dirty clothes in the hamper, clean clothes in drawers or closets, etc. Take it step by step .If you can count, you can teach.

> **BE SPECIFIC.** If you are one of those people who think a bed isn't made properly unless you can bounce a quarter off it, then you better be prepared to divulge the secrets of just exactly how to accomplish that task. Breaking the

The Nature Of Children

process down into steps works well for this kind of situation, too.

SHORT-CUT PROBLEM AREAS. If Julie is having a problem being nice to her brother, break her day down into individual activities rather than nag her consistently to "get along." Explain *how* we act riding in the car, *how* we behave at the table, *how* we "share" a chore or a treat without digressing into a brawl. And *why* it is important to you for her to act this way. Make each activity a "mini lesson" in itself, with appropriate rewards or consequences for each session. Give her every opportunity to succeed, rather than pronouncing one final judgment at the end whether it has been a good day, or not. Children who consistently have bad days need to "redirect" themselves by collecting some good moments. A few moments, they can handle... a day could seem like forever.

AVOID UNNECESSARY DEMANDS. Remember what your children are capable of and be flexible if a system isn't working. Admit it, and try something different. Different methods work for different kids even if they live in the same family.

USE "NO" AND "DON'T" SPARINGLY. If you can't think of a good reason to say no, then don't. Reserve these "rank pullers" for the big stuff. An over-use of them causes children to become "hard of hearing" and you to become bossy instead of the boss.

The future is an ever-changing place and all of our children are headed there. The problems and challenges they meet will not be the same as when we first came on the scene. Our world was bigger—less people, less technology, less deterioration of our environment and our planet. The "good old days" were closer for the simple fact that the rate of change was slower than it is now, or will ever be, again. For these reasons alone, it becomes imperative that we raise the standard of our children's development to match the new and changing times.

We can do this by raising our own standards of deciding how and what we will teach them to get by on. Then we have to "make it a point" to accomplish it. If we can do that, we will be instilling in them one of the most valuable assets humanity has to offer… the ability to "pave the way" for someone else. That's the highest level of human nature there is.

And that's the point.

9

Safeguards

Protection is one of the most important priorities in today's societies. Whether you find yourself at the top or bottom end of the income scale, programs that provide security against all manner of unexpected occurrences are available to you. Some are even funded by the government for people who have no income at all. Most of these programs have been around long enough for a person to be considered unwise if they don't participate in them. Such as insurance. In the same way, the role of today's modern parent is different from past generations, in that it has been modified to include not only "bringing home the bread," but also providing some guarantee that nothing will happen to it. And we pay an exorbitant price to assure this.

But along with exorbitant prices, have come exorbitant demands.

What is "humanly possible" is no longer a consideration. Something made even more obvious by the high cost of court proceedings and medical care. During the Revolution, a great many of our patriots spent their own personal funds to foot the bill, and afterward, many of the common people lost property because they couldn't come up with their share of the taxes to cover our newfound political processes and expenses. That is a far cry from today, where our recent casualties of September Eleventh have been partly compensated by the government simply for people having been "in the wrong place at the wrong time." It is not a question of right or wrong. Our "Uncle Sam" has simply come into more money over the years, and his sympathies have changed accordingly. And so it is with families.

Families today have a great capacity to give nearly anything they desire to their children. Very few of them go to bed each night cold, or wondering where their next meal will come from — much less worried over the political state of the world. At the same time, we are faced with a growing number of up and coming citizens who feel surprisingly little personal responsibility toward any of these things. Logic tells us that people who have all things provided for them, should then be free to provide for others. So, what's the problem?

Human nature doesn't agree.

That's because before we are finely tuned governments, before we are societies, before we are even families: *we are human*. All of us. And we are not responsible for the nature that is inherent in any of us. It is what has caused us to survive over the years. Humans figured out some way to get by after the Revolution: it's a fact proven by the obvious evidence that we — as Americans — are still around. Similarly, they have proven equally resilient to the many changes that have come along since.

It is human nature to survive. To build up protective strongholds for one's self and one's family is one of the most intensely driven forces in life. That is why it is essential for the success of any family, to have this force working *for* and not against them. Insecurity breeds discontent in both parents and children. Especially in children. But as insurmountable as many of the issues that adults often have to face may seem, it's nice to know that a child's world is – for the most part – easily secured.

That is, as long as a few vital truths are not overlooked. The most important being that—unlike adults—children are in a constant state of change. In a brief fifteen to twenty years, they will go through more physical, mental, and emotional change than the next fifty years that follow. During that time, there are monumental stages they will pass through before crossing over the threshold of adulthood. The truth is, what will be enough security for the infant will not always suffice for a ten-year-old, which will in turn not hold sufficient for a mature, healthy teen. Since parents often have a tendency to overlook the fact that their darlings are actually growing up, it is beneficial to take a closer look at the stages.

PHYSICAL — Infant to Five

These are the years when the majority of a child's security will come from physical care. And as much as overworked parents who feel inundated with diapers, mealtimes, bath-times and bedtimes will often beg to differ, they are the years that require the least from the parent, as far as security goes. Children at this stage are easily soothed, quickly diverted, and in open, total awe of their parents. They are oblivious of social or monetary standing… that is, unless a parent makes it a point to intrude into their protective innocence of such things. This is the only time in childhood when a parent —no matter what IQ level or worldly achievements may be—is perfectly capable of meeting every need of their child.

MENTAL – Six to Fourteen

> *It is still possible for the parent to be a hero.*

When a child enters the school years, he slows down a little physically, and his brain begins to become more and more demanding. Not only of himself, but of the things around him. "How does this work?" "Why is that so?" And the all-engrossing personal quest: "How can I get Mom to agree to this?" Here's when they begin to ask you things you're not prepared for, and – when you least expect it – catch you in some embarrassing mistakes.

Their physical world has expanded to include not only school, but their friends' houses and families as well. And their brain, which will never be quite as busy as it will at this age, begins to compare people, places and things at a furious rate. Although mom and dad are still held in high regard, they are studying them very carefully, now. It is still possible for the parent to be a hero at this stage… but the kids are definitely keeping score.

MORAL — Fifteen to Twenty

By this stage, many children are way beyond their parents, both mentally and physically. This is due mainly because we now live in an age of accelerated information. A time when the majority of our jobs are not physically demanding. A few generations ago, a youth of eighteen was no match for a fully mature man in his thirties who did anything physical for a living. Nowadays, a father who works at an office every day would be hard-pressed to best his son at arm wrestling:

The Nature Of Children

especially if that son is a school sports hero. But luckily, the youth has his sights zeroed in on maturity at this point and the mental and physical aspects of life now begin to take a backseat for a while.

To conquer and achieve *something of value* becomes the new driving force at this – and only this – time in life when the whole wide world is open to him. The only security a parent can give at this point is approval, which is the last thing lacking in the ability of the youth to provide security of his own. This is when the heart steps forward to make demands, for it is craving *cause and reason...* something—or someone —to live for.

These three stages of a child's development are linked together by transitional years and there are always those who develop faster or slower than others. It is interesting to note how much time is spent hurrying or slowing down our children when the process makes absolutely no difference in achieving adulthood. The destination is the same either way. Whether one matured early, or late, is never a prerequisite to the business world. Still, the consideration of the developmental stages of childhood helps to understand what is—or isn't—needed at a certain age.

For example, a child in stage one who is afraid of the dark, is easily calmed by the presence of a parent. The same fear for a child in stage two, would also require an explanation and assurance. If you have a teen who still has this problem, there are bigger things than the "boogeyman" to be dealt with. It comes down to approving (or disapproving) of what they are *really* doing with their time.

Following are a few things you can do to help your children feel more protected and secure, no matter what's going on in the world around them.

> **STICK TO A ROUTINE.** Especially for the little ones. This gives a child a "sense" of order in a world that is so often confusing.
>
> **GIVE HONEST ANSWERS TO HONEST QUESTIONS.** This promotes trust in authority, which can be a real asset if carried over into adulthood.
>
> **DON'T SAY TOO MUCH.** Children learn too much too early, these days, and often miss out on some of the peace and contentment of childhood. Try not to argue or discuss things in front of them with other adults that don't concern them, or burden them with overly descriptive information on things they are simply not ready for.
>
> **GIVE THEM RESPONSIBILITY** at an early age. Even a toddler can be responsible for something (such as picking up toys). If you wait until you think they are old enough—or until it's convenient—they will feel left out and start looking for your attention in other ways. Children crave attention, and if they can't get your approval in some way or another... they'll settle for disapproval.
>
> **SHOULDER YOUR PARENTAL BURDENS WITH DIGNITY.** Never allow yourself to whine or complain to your children how much you do or give up for them. And above all, never make them feel like they owe you something for it. You have already been "paid" for your

sacrifices: somebody gave the same for you at that age.

REMIND THEM HOW IMPORTANT THEY ARE. Telling a child how important they are, to you, provides the emotional stability that security thrives on. It is the strong thread that holds the family together, no matter what that family goes through.

DON'T HOLD THEM BACK. If you have a child that matures early... let them go. A child that is allowed to reach for the highest level of their capabilities, gains confidence, and a sense of belonging in the scheme of things.

All these things are "safeguards" for today's families, and —like insurance—can protect against the insecurity and instability of our modern times. In a day when we no longer have to hunt our own food, plant our own crops or build our own houses, it is sometimes difficult to figure out not only what success is, but what a person can be successful at. And with so many activities for a child to choose from out there, it is becoming more and more common to slip through childhood without taking enough time at any one thing to become good at it. Life can be a bewildering journey if you don't know where or how far you're going with it. It can be downright shaky...

Unless you put up a few safeguards.

10

Family Law

Everyone needs the law. Those who break it, those of us who don't, and those who make a living by explaining the differences between these two groups. A person does not have to understand or even know the law to be subject to it. But there is no doubt that a clear understanding of these things makes for a more secure—and more responsible—citizen. The same is true within families.

Families are an individual's first experience with group behavior. And it should be every family's goal to raise up individuals who will be self-disciplined enough to never have to brush up against that longer and often unyielding arm of our society's laws. Being "brought to task" as an adult has far reaching effects that are sometimes impossible to get out from under. That's why it is vital in early years to develop the respect and discipline it takes to "order ourselves" before we get there.

> *Families are an individual's first experience with group behaviour.*

"Law awareness" is not something parents have to purposefully set out to cover in their list of *"Goals I would like to Accomplish in Raising My Children.*" It is something they do naturally. A person's attitudes and methods in dealing with the law will be conveyed to their children, simply because children will take on their attitudes and methods of dealing with things. That old saying "Do as I say and not as I do," is a fallacy. Though it might bring a few moments of peace during a fleeting argument (only because you are bigger than them), it is faithfully creating a piece of yourself within their character, even as you speak. Children will always do as you do before they do as you say. That's human nature. And this is something that can work for them or against them in life.

Every family has laws, whether they have put a name to them or not. And every family spends whatever time it takes to enforce these. The differences lie in how you choose to do it and there is no doubt that some methods are more successful than others. It is not unusual to walk through a public place and see a full-blown issue being tried out in family court, no matter who happens to be passing by. You do not have to stay longer than fifteen minutes in the toy department of any store to prove this. And even if you have your darlings trained up well enough not to crumble under these temptations, there are two to every one of yours that don't.

That's because humans have a driving force to voice and debate their opinions and it starts at a very early age. Children could spend most of their time doing this if you would let them, but as an adult, there are a few other things that demand your attention now and again, as well as your kids. Besides that, it's embarrassing.

So what do you do with this fiery little piece of humanity we're forced to deal with day in and day out? Do your best to keep it under control and hope by the time they reach voting age they have developed some sort of wisdom—or at least a little common sense— through the process of osmosis? Possibly. There are a lot of young adults released out into the world every day with only "some sort of wisdom, or a little common sense" to get along on.

Invariably it makes for unnecessary troubles in the adult world that would have been far less painful to learn in the less threatening environment of the home they just came out of. But if **Wisdom** and **Common Sense** are two of the most important things you can give a child, how do you go about teaching them? The secret here is to look at yourself.

How much advice have you ever taken from others?

Probably not much compared to what you have learned through your own experiences. A lot goes into the willingness to trust in someone else's opinions rather than your own. Nine times out of ten it is a relationship thing and not so much what someone says but who they are that makes the difference. Which is as it should be. That's human nature. And children are no different. Wonderful things can come from learning to handle one's own behavior, but – like a shotgun – it can cause some damage when misfired. If fired at too close a range it can literally blow someone away.

The best and most proven method of dealing with these situations is one that goes back thousands of years. It's called the **Family Conference** and goes as far back though humanity as you would care to trace. It has hung around this long because it works. Here are some characteristics that differentiate the Family Conference from other types of family gatherings:

* The whole family is involved.

* Every member has a vote.

* Every member has a right to be heard without being criticized.

* Problems are aired and settled here by a majority rule.

* In order to participate in this activity, **Rules of Conduct** must be strictly adhered to.

The Family Conference is one more great way to turn your family time into "prime time" simply because it sets a specific time to deal with things you deal with anyway. The difference is, it channels the "line of fire" to go off at appropriate targets instead of the isles of department stores where someone could sustain injuries. A child that wants to know exactly *why* he can't have an official fire-breathing, missile shooting, electronic version of some character of the latest hit-movie, might take the answer "Because it costs too much money!" as a personal insult. Like maybe he's not worth that much money. Or worse yet, he is worth *less* than the price of a mere toy.

Even if you were the first to insist this isn't true (no matter what mood, you're in), he probably won't even bring it up as an argument. Because the clock is running. And he only has a certain amount of time to win or lose this thing. So, he's going to take his best shot. Which is the hope that you would rather get it than argue about it, then work the details out later. Besides, how many times has that ever worked for him?

At least once, or he wouldn't be going for it, again.

The Family Conference is a non-threatening environment

for settling these kind of disputes without squashing hope and self-esteem to do it. That doesn't mean you whip out your copy of "*Robert's Rules of Order*" and hold a Family Conference right there in the middle of the store. You make a little adjustment in the way you respond to the situation.

A response of "What a toy! I can see why you would want one of these. But it's pretty expensive, isn't it? To spend this much money, we'd have to talk about it first at Family Conference. Maybe you should bring it up, tonight." Which defers the decision until later, he still has the hope that he might actually get one, and he has something important to contribute to the group around the conference table.

You mean you really might actually have to buy this thing? Not necessarily. But if it's that important to him, you may have to set up a way that he could earn it (through behavior, chores, allowance, etc.), and then follow through with the plan. But you would be surprised how many of these episodes are no more than passing fancies, which when placed with a value of actual time, effort, or money to get... are not worth it. Even in the child's eyes.

Which puts the decision making experience back in his corner. That's the only place it's going to do him any good, anyway. Hopefully, you've already had more than your share of those experiences in your own life and knew the minute you saw the thing it wasn't worth half the price they were asking for it.

The Family Conference allows you to pour all your "spur of the moment" problems into a time slot that you are best equipped to deal with it in. Experience shows that people deal a lot better with things they are prepared for than things they aren't. Even though the Family Conference has the characteristics mentioned above, it is something you can successfully mold to your own family's routine to get the fullest benefit from.

If you are a young family, and spend significant time during each day settling disputes and maintaining control, you might need to have one every evening. If you have older children whose problems or concerns tend to come up mostly if they want to do or get something, your conferences can be more occasional.

Ultimately the habit of Family Conference will carry over even into the adult years, when it is still the desire of the grown children to seek counsel from their parents and each other to face life's many challenges, thereby avoiding some of the mistakes so many of us have had to deal with on our own. One family member can learn from another the hazards of owing thousands of dollars to credit agencies without personally having to go through the unpleasant experience themselves, if only we would be honest enough to share these things with each other.

However you set up your schedule for Family Conference, here are some of the basic rules that will make each conference time more beneficial to everyone:

> **EVERY FAMILY MEMBER'S OPINION IS IMPORTANT.** Schedule Family Conferences so that all the family members can be present to participate. Unless Dad or big brother are off fighting the third world war, this isn't impossible and should be a major priority.
>
> **DO NOT INTERRUPT.** Everyone will get a chance to be

heard and it is not acceptable to talk when someone else is voicing an opinion.

If you have a complaint to make about someone, you must **SAY THREE NICE THINGS** about them, first. Offsetting negative criticisms by positive remarks guards against attitudes that can undermine relationships. If a person cannot do this, then he is being too selfish or narrow-minded about the situation and is not ready to bring it before the group with a reasonable attitude toward working things out. So, the issue will be deferred for discussion until that time.

LET THE MAJORITY RULE when it comes to deciding consequences for certain behaviors or establishing new rules for things. You will find the group amazingly fair because they know the same power could be wielded against them, next time. This is a good example of a "mini-democracy."

DON'T HAVE FAMILY CONFERENCES DURING MEAL TIMES. Matters brought to the conference table can often be emotional and probing, and should never impose on the comfort and security of mealtimes.

OPEN A COMPLAINT DEPARTMENT. If you have young children who find it difficult to wait until the rest of the family comes home to settle something, let them write (or you write for them) out a complaint and put it in a box. Assure them that these things will be discussed, first, at the Family Conference and they will feel the security of something "tangible" to prove this.

Putting Family Conferences into effect in your home will strengthen your security level. Children will begin to trust that their important issues will be dealt with fairly and they will feel empowered in the sense that they are a necessary ingredient to the process. They will put more thought in coming to their opinions simply because they appreciate that their opinions matter. And sometimes they will amaze you with their ability to shoulder their part of "family law." They will become adept at negotiating and listening to others and learn that putting fairness into practice benefits everyone. That's how you open your door to **Wisdom** and **Common Sense**. And when these two start showing up at your Family Conference table...

Then you've made it.

11

Let The House Rule

Even in this age of permissiveness, there are some rules that parents will never change their minds about. Toddlers who want to play in the street, preschoolers who insist on staying out after midnight, or ten-year-olds who demand to live on sweets until they are fifteen, have little or no chance at winning when they bring these kind of requests up before a fairly normal parent. Yet, it is not uncommon to see out-and-out battles over these things in public places. No doubt, because the only thing children have going for them in these situations, is a parent's reluctance to make a public spectacle of themselves.

So, why does it happen over and over? Because two of the strongest influences on human nature are at work here. ***Impulse*** and ***Temptation***. Conflicts with these two things run from the beginning of life to the end of it and maturity is often judged by how well a person has gained control over them. Some people never do. And some very gifted people, who—by all indications— should be wildly successful at something, actually miss the mark of their destinies because of their inabilities to cope with these things.

History proves that successful people spring from all walks of life. It makes no difference if one is rich or poor, male or female, or even from one culture or another. But the thing that all successful people do have in common is that they have learned to control Impulse and Temptation.

Some families have been able to hand the "keys" to their success down to their children but even this is no guarantee that the heir will be able to drive the thing home because—in the end —success is an individual thing and we are all required to make the journey, ourselves, no matter how much advice we get. The secret to dealing successfully with these situations is not to correct your children for the impulses and temptations they have, but rather allow them to experience the consequences for the choices they make when faced with them. This produces "response-ability." And the more opportunities a child has to respond to something, the quicker they will learn the best way to handle it.

If it is true that what a person learns in childhood stays with them all their life, and that at no other time will a person learn as quickly or absorb so much; then the most important of life's lessons should be dealt with in childhood. Children should be given every opportunity to taste and handle impulse and temptation, to make their own decisions, and to realize the consequences of their own choices.

Does this mean you should suffer through an agonizing month of letting that ten-year-old eat nothing but junk and hope his own natural functions will eventually make him crave vegetables and salads once in a while? Not at all. Life's consequences are final. There are many things which would produce devastating effects in our children's future if we were to let loose their ignorance and vulnerability out in it too soon. But like the astronaut who has flown countless simulated space missions before he actually "blasts off," parents can begin training their children for the race long before they ever enter it.

To do this, takes some role-playing. Let's look first at the role of the parent. As a parent, you are not Fate. It is not your duty to decide what your children will do and then force or coerce them into doing it. Nor is it your place to pit yourself against them as a sparring partner, in order for them to learn better how to "deal with things" in life. You are the wise counselor—the advocate—who is ever on their side through this great trial and always available for advice when they need it. You are not the judge, for then you would have to be impartial, and it goes against human nature to be impartial with one's own children. Besides that, the greatest influence over a child is a parent, and vice-versa. There is an automatic conflict whenever these two things are placed opposite of each other. The trick is to avoid getting into that position.

Now, let's switch our attention to the child. The most important thing to remember about the child's role in this scenario is that – to them – this is not a game. It is real. To quote a famous source, children *"…believe all things, hope all things, and endure all things."* They are at the same time vulnerable and resilient. To have the greatest impact during the "teachable moments" you will be encountering during these simulations, you must remember to – at all times – treat them with the utmost respect as a person. In the same way that most children are born with healthy hearts, lungs, and other vital organs that are fully functional at birth, they also – contrary to popular opinion – come equipped with fully developed emotions. To insult or criticize them personally for their decisions will undermine not only your efforts to train them but your relationship with them, as well.

In life there are certain things an individual has no control over. Such as death and taxes, along with the many things our society has set down as requirements for peaceful living. Whether or not a person believes in these things has no bearing on them. They are non-negotiable. We abide by the rules, or we pay the fines. Everything seems to cost but fairness is not an issue here. That's life. So, if it is our goal to model our disciplines to best train up our children for life, then the best family training situation is to have "house rules."

The rules of the house are non-negotiable, in the same way that life is, and the consequences for breaking them should be made very clear. In this way, the responsibility stays with the child to make the right decisions and grapple with the consequences, himself, if he chooses wrong. Because parents have given the authority of these rules over to the house, they are not in a position to pardon an offense or change the rules with each new situation.

In this way, they can remain sympathetic to their children during these times without giving anger or resentment the ability to block relationships. It is much more difficult for a child to project their displeasure toward a parent who had nothing to do with his decision in the first place. Nine times out of ten, they will seek the parent's solace, or assistance for a way out. And if they do...

Give them one. But make it an acceptable solution – or better yet – two or three options the child can choose from. It is not the purpose of house rules to create the prison mentality of crime and punishment. It is to teach children to *successfully* deal with their problems. In order to do that, you have to "set them up" to succeed.

For instance, if Johnny has ventured into a friend's house whose parents are not home, and it is a "house rule" that there must always be adult supervision in order to play inside, Mom does not have to take it as a personal challenge to her authority in order to deal with it. She can even express sympathy that he must now choose one of the consequences (that he knows beforehand, so there is no "power-struggle" for a lesser sentence) that the house rule requires.

These might include a restriction of playing with that friend for a specified time, several house chores as penance, early bedtime, or whatever else you and your children have agreed upon as an appropriate consequence when the house rule was made. Once the "fine" has been paid, let it be paid in full. If you agreed that this was an appropriate consequence before it actually happened, it is unfair and unethical for you to show anger or disappointment after the child has "paid his dues."

Nagging about it after the fact will cause a lack of respect for you, not the rule, as well as a lack of self-confidence in the child when it comes to making decisions. Remember, the most important thing for the child is your relationship. If there is a rift in that, all learning stops until it is resolved.

House rules can relieve a lot of the everyday tensions and disagreements that rob families of quality time together. By delegating the burden of your non-negotiable rules to the house, you can have more time and energy for meaningful communications over issues that really matter. The proper use of house rules strengthens relationships and establishes and affirms family values. Children are more secure if they know what is expected of them and more independent if they are allowed to make choices. Following are some guidelines for setting up house rules that will help you in establishing your own.

- Make sure your **HOUSE RULES ARE NON-NEGOTIABLE**. Bedtimes do not come under this category because they change with the interruptions of daily schedules and with the ages of individual children. On the other hand, behavior at bedtime can be incorporated into a house rule (if this is a problem area for you) because you can decide beforehand what the desired behavior is, and what the consequences will be if it is not followed.

- **DON'T MAKE TOO MANY**. Too many rules can bog anybody down so try to stick to the ones that are most important to you. Pick and choose the problem areas you want to deal with and don't set yourself up to be the perfect family overnight. Remember, "practice makes perfect," and the only way to get there is to endure the mistakes and mishaps along the way.

- **PROVIDE CHOICES WHEN SETTING DOWN CONSEQUENCES**. This lets the debate rest with which choice the child will make for his infraction, as opposed to protesting against having any consequence at all. A simple "Shall you choose, or should I?" almost always results in cooperation, simply because a disagreeable choice is better than no choice, at all.

> *Consistency is the strongest form of discipline there is.*

STICK TO YOUR RULES. If you don't get into the habit of enforcing the house rules and slip back into bickering over every incident, again, they won't be much help to you.

LET YOUR CHILDREN PARTICIPATE in setting down the rules and consequences. That way, they will carry more weight and leave less room for argument, later, because they helped to establish them. Arguments are easily quelled with "We made that a house rule, remember? We don't change those."

DON'T CHANGE THE RULES. If you agreed to the consequences when the rules were set down, you should never add anything to them because you were "really upset about it" when it actually happened. Consistency is the strongest form of discipline there is, not anger.

House rules are another way to help turn your family time into quality time. So, the next time your children get into a royal battle while you're making dinner and it takes fifteen minutes to settle who started it... don't. Make it a house rule that fighting brings a consequence to both participants.

Then let the house rule.

Part Two:

Changing Behavior

The Structure

    12. The Great Controversy
    13. Personality Plus
    14. Choice Cuts
    15. The Winner's Circle

The Program

    16. Phase One
    17. Phase Two
    18. Phase Three

The Structure

12

The Great Controversy

Most parents will use the same method of discipline with their children that their own parents used with them, whether it was good or bad. In recent years, there has been great controversy about the effectiveness—and sometimes even the morality—of the various methods. Some of those methods our society has even stepped into homes and schools to regulate. To spank, or not to spank? It's a decision that involves many elements and careful contemplation of not only the parent's perspective but also the child's.

There is no debate over the fact that children need to be corrected: some more frequently than others. Parents will also generally agree that what works well for one of their children will not always have the same effect on another. But no matter what method you choose, consistency and follow-through are the two most important ingredients to insure success.

If Jenny gets a spanking for running into the street one time, it should be the same if it happens again. Similarly, if you threaten a spanking if she does, you better follow through and deliver should she decide to put your words to the test. It is the nature of children to test limits. But it is also the nature of children to accept those limits if they are clearly defined. Consistency and follow-through not only saves on frustrations and confrontations in the long run, it provides the benefit of a sense of security for the child, as well. Though it may take more time and effort in the beginning, it actually becomes easier later on.

Is it worth the time to make this "investment of discipline" in the long run? You bet it is. Because no matter how you decide to handle it, parenting, itself, is for the long run anyway. And the most efficient method of instruction is always the clearest, no matter how complicated or simple it is. The three most popular methods of discipline are time out, restriction of privileges, and spanking. Let's take a closer look at each of these, and the benefits or drawbacks that they present.

Time Out

This is the most effective method of correction for younger children for the following reasons. It is immediate, it is uncomfortable, and it gets quick results. The difficulties that "time outs" sometimes impose are usually with a child's inability to handle inactivity (especially for those with hyperactive disorders), and the occasional circumstance where there is no place to remove the child from the current activity in order to carry it out.

Restriction of Privileges

Restriction of privileges works better for older rather than younger children for the simple reason that the consequences of the misconduct are delayed. A younger child who has to wait until tomorrow or next week to forfeit a favorite activity must be old enough to know how far away next week is, or at least able to remember a misbehavior from one day to the next. If there is not sufficient recall to contemplate or anticipate the cost, the method loses impact.

However, restriction of privileges does give children the lesson of personally having to "pay" for their own mistakes. The drawback to this method is the propensity for parents to withdraw things that are not relative to the "crime" without taking enough thought as to the "after-effects" on their children. It is also common to use this correction device too frequently. Sadly, there are many children that spend the greater portion of their free time perpetually "grounded."

Spanking

If you are a parent with a tendency to display anger when correcting your child—much less if you have an anger problem in general—you should not resort to spanking. It's true that this form of correction gets the most immediate, long-term results but it has some dangerous pitfalls to watch out for. While it is beneficial to show disapproval toward certain behaviors, it is never beneficial to show anger toward your child as a person. This kind of negative feedback almost always produces feelings of inadequacy and low self-esteem later on.

It is also true that improper forms of physical correction (such as unexpected smacks, overly hard ones, or such punishments for inconsistent reasons) shows disrespect to a child as a human being. Unfairness causes some of the deepest wounds in children and has much the same result an adult would have toward an employer that was illegally docking his pay.

To inflict physical discomfort for any reason can only work if it is justified. Without this, it will produce a similar effect to blowing an electric fuse: any power and light that was desired in the first place (which should be the aim of all forms of discipline) is reduced to a confusion of darkness and chaos until the proper "circuits" are restored.

There are parents that have achieved high levels of good behavior in their children without ever having spanked them. At the same time, there are parents that consistently spank who have consistently ill-behaved kids. The secret to any method of discipline is to find the right method for the individual. That's because discipline is a relationship, not a philosophy. The best forms of discipline are the ones that promote mutual love and respect between parent and child.

Here is a "checklist" to measure the accuracy of disciplinary methods, to help you decide if you should "readjust" some of yours, or maybe even change them completely.

> **WHAT ARE THE RESULTS?** How does your child feel toward you after being corrected? Do your "applications" sufficiently cut down or get rid of the undesired behavior?

> **HOW DO YOU FEEL AFTERWARD?** Do you have frequent regrets for being too harsh or unthoughtful toward your child? Do you ever over-indulge them in other ways to make up for it?

DO YOU CONSISTENTLY STRUGGLE WITH THE SAME UNWANTED BEHAVIORS in spite of frequent discipline?

DOES YOUR CHILD FREQUENTLY LIE OR AVOID YOU as opposed to making an effort to follow rules?

IS YOUR CHILD DISRESPECTFUL TOWARD YOU?

DO YOU EVER FEEL RESENTMENT at having to deal with the inappropriate behaviors of your children?

If you had some unexpected time off, **WOULD YOU RATHER DO SOMETHING WITH YOUR CHILDREN, OR SPEND SOME QUIET TIME BY YOURSELF**

DO YOUR CHILDREN MORE FREQUENTLY EXASPERATE OR EMBARRASS you rather than make you proud?

If you are not happy with your answers to two or more of these questions, your current method of discipline needs some adjusting. If you are unhappy or dissatisfied with most of them, then you

> *Good parenting makes life good.*

need to try something new altogether. Whatever you do, don't give in to the temptation to feel disappointed at having to change or make changes.

Instead, be encouraged that you are sensitive and dedicated enough to being a successful parent to realize the need. Because most parents never do. Which is a sad statistic considering that children are the most forgiving and resilient members of the human race. What's more, the effects of experiencing forgiveness and resiliency have far-reaching benefits to the development of human character. Finding a method of discipline that works for both you and your child is good parenting.

And good parenting makes life good.

13

Personality Plus

Considering the number of personality types there are within the human race, it is no wonder that a method of discipline that works for one child, will not always work for another. Parents continually marvel that children born of the same family can be so vastly different from each other. And in this day where many of our modern families consist of a mixture of "yours, mine, and ours," we should not be surprised that the parenting process has taken on new complexities. It is not uncommon to have within the same family, a child that will persist in bad behavior no matter how many spankings he gets, and another that will crumble and never do the thing again, when you simply cast a "firm eye" in her direction.

The answer to this mystery is for the parent to discern the differences in each child, then adjust the methods accordingly. Which takes time. And awareness. Both of which can only come about by accurate observation of how your children react to various situations. It takes a closer look than simply noticing that your children "fight about something every night when you are in the middle of making dinner." Is your routine simply to yell, "Knock it off!" from the kitchen and go on with your preparations, only to face the same fiasco tomorrow? Many do. Or, do they successfully drag you away from the chore to be the grand moderator of yet another dispute?

However you choose to deal with the problem, the secret to success in this situation is to realize that the nightly arguing is not the real problem. The real problem is attention. For some reason, your children feel they are not getting enough from you: whether the observation is accurate, or not. It is sometimes comforting to parents to point out here, that eighty percent of the time this observation from their children is not accurate.

But that doesn't make it any less of a problem.

> **Attention is respect.**

The answer? Give them more attention. But before you say, "How in the world can I, when I have to keep up with a full time job, the meals, the house, etc." Let's take a closer look at what attention really is. Attention is respect. That doesn't mean you have to stop your dinner preparations in order to give in to their desire to control your time. At the same time, it doesn't mean that you should use the perpetual ignoring routine on them, either. Knowing your children well enough and taking the time to find out the best way to deal with their particular personalities, is having respect for them as individuals. No matter how old they are. And that kind of attention is what they are really after.

Do you have a child that is constantly "needling" the others? Do you have one that can't sit still long enough to let you get anything done? Or maybe you have a child that spends so much time in his room with video games, you're lucky you can even get him to come to dinner. Each of these is a different symptom of the same problem: a lack of attention. Let's fix the attention problem by looking at each of these "types" of children in a different way.

The "Needler"

This type of child is a very social person who—when they can't get positive feedback from people— will settle for negative, simply to maintain interaction. This is a child who needs to be constantly participating in something. They need frequent, if not constant, recognition. The solution? More responsibility. This kind of child makes a wonderful helper, and thrives on the satisfaction of not only mastering new tasks, but in doing things for others, too.

This type of child will not respond well to either a time out method of discipline, or spanking. The quickest and most beneficial discipline for the "needler" is to get an immediate consequence for their behavior that incorporates their full attention and energy. They need a chore. To have him set the table, make the salad, or unload the dishwasher, not only removes him from the group temporarily (time out), it gives him something to do. Which was what he needed in the first place.

It also allows him to pay for his infraction (spanking) in order to release his feelings of inadequacy. What's more, if you will take the opportunity, here, to praise him for doing a good job (rather than responding, "… and you'll get another one if you bother anybody, again!"), you'll even get a change in attitude. Which is an all-time "biggie" on any parent list.

The Hyperactive

In the same way the "needler" needs something to do, the "hyperactive" child needs something to do, too... but for different reasons. This kind of child is driven more by physical energy than social need. While he may not bother others during a group television time, he might quietly (and often thoughtlessly) pull the stuffing out of a hole in the upholstery while he is watching the show.

In early years, this type of child tends to be the climber or explorer variety. They often send parents to their "wits end" having to deal with some of the situations they can get into. Later on (and especially if they have a teacher that is not adept at handling this kind of behavior), they are often in frequent trouble at school.

Once again, time out and spanking are merely opportunities for the escalation of bad behaviors for these types of children. And once again, they need to be doing something. But unlike the child who merely needs social approval, the hyperactive child needs to be at the edge of physical endurance most of the time. The consequence of a chore needs to be more physical for them; such as taking out the trash (which constitutes a trip outside), carrying laundry, or scrubbing pots and pans.

This child thrives not so much on approval as being needed. Praise for a difficult achievement is more important to them than a job well done. A change of attitude comes for these children not from approval, but from a sudden need that only they can fulfill. A wise parent will take notice when their hyperactive child is on the verge of "erring" and come up with a "sudden need" beforehand.

The Withdrawn

This type of child lives in "a world of their own." They are not driven by either social or physical desires but rather take solace in their own active imaginations. They are mentally ahead of most children, yet, they often fall into the category of what educators call "mentally lazy"... which is a highly inadequate term. The fact is these children are not lazy, they are bored. If they neglect mundane schoolwork or a parent's urgent call, it is only because they are actively, and mentally, engaged in more thrilling things. This type of child needs to be inspired and challenged.

Time out is the most effective method of discipline for the "withdrawn" child, simply because the experience of being removed from an engaging pastime is almost unbearable for them. As they grow older, the restriction of privileges serves the same purpose. But there is a note of warning here: these types of children are easily offended. And too many offenses can lead to deep resentments. The attitudes of the withdrawn child are well guarded, and often mistaken for stubborn or "hard-headedness" when it is really that most wonderful attribute of determination bound up under lock and key.

All children need discipline, not only to learn the rules and be kept under control, but to feel secure. They need authority. But authority does not always mean who can yell the loudest and have the last word. Or being the one who can physically force them to do something. True authority

> *Intelligence is not interchangeable with authority.*

wears the cap of wisdom. There are a lot of children in our society who are smarter than their parents in many ways. Surprisingly, it makes little difference. Intelligence is not interchangeable with authority. It is something we are born into as opposed to earning. And as history proves, it is often the office of authority that causes a ruler to grow, as opposed to the road to getting there. The same is true with parenting.

It is the nature of children to be very forgiving and resilient individuals. And as stated before, their ability to have faith and trust in the individuals who care for them, sometimes surpasses the capacity of adults when put to similar tests. That's a wonderful thing. Nature allows us to "grow up together" with our children by starting things off with the simplest of interactions: food, shelter, and handling. And by the time they're old enough to judge you, you've had more than enough space to figure things out.

Nevertheless, discipline—of any kind—is often so uncomfortable for parent and child that it is put off as a very last resort. Some families even ignore the issue completely, believing that out of sight is truly out of mind. Something that usually refers to the child's mind, not the parent's. That's because few children who have no rules, take it upon themselves to go by any.

So, here are a few pointers on discipline to help those parents whose methods are doing a better job of wearing them out, more than keeping their children in line:

> Any form of **DISCIPLINE SHOULD HAVE A POSITIVE OUTCOME.** If the majority of your confrontations with your children end in either you or them being more upset than when you started out... it's time to make some

changes.

If you are not seeing any changes in unwanted behaviors after consistently applied efforts in that area, **DON'T BE AFRAID TO TRY SOMETHING ELSE.**

Don't worry about "being fair" in the eyes of other siblings. If Sarah gets a spanking for doing something, and her sister merely gets sent to her room for the same infraction two days later, **POINT OUT THE OUTCOME OF THE METHODS INSTEAD OF THE METHODS THEMSELVES**. A simple response of, "Wouldn't it be nice if that's all it took for you to behave, too?" is enough to make your point.

LET YOUR WORD BE YOUR BOND. If you say it, do it. When your children know where your "bottom line" is, they will stop trying to find it all the time.

DON'T HOLD GRUDGES. When an incident is over and paid for, it's over. Never give your children the "silent treatment" for hours or days on end, or remind them of all their infractions long afterward. This makes for low self-esteem and sometimes feelings of rejection that can take years to mend. If ever.

LISTEN TO YOUR INSTINCTS. Don't be in a hurry to take the advice of others if you "don't feel quite right" about doing it. Parents really do have a built-in sense of what's best for their own children and sometimes an outsider only sees the tip of the iceberg when it comes to the real reasons for your child's behavior.

ALWAYS END ON A POSITIVE NOTE. Make sure things get "back to normal" between you and your child as quickly as possible after a confrontation. Never let them go to bed or off to school with feelings of resentment or guilt. Reassure them that you love them—no matter what—and simply want what's best for them. And insist on a similar response from them. If there are lingering negative feelings between you, there is still something to be worked out. Habits of good or bad communication begin in the formative years: and it is as important for them to not hold grudges as it is for you. Because the quality of their future is at stake.

Discipline is like electricity: there is both a negative and a positive charge. As with all forces of nature, the secret to getting any benefit from it is in how well you can control it. One of the great fallacies in today's homes is that discipline and authority have to be accompanied by a display of anger in order to carry any weight. This is not true. Anger is a negative thing that produces negative results. When choosing between negative and positive, positive is always better.

There are many wonderful books on the market that offer step-by-step instructions on positive discipline and most of them will do the job. The bottom line in choosing is to decide if it will have positive results for you and your family. Why is it so important to be positive? Because it's like the difference between light and dark: children naturally gravitate toward the light.

It's human nature.

14

Choice Cuts

The old saying "life is choices" never meant so much as in today's society where we have so many things to choose from. Often, we spend the largest portion of our time looking at the options instead of actually picking one. Many are the nights when we finally come to the conclusion that there is nothing on TV only after we have spent more time than we like to admit "surfing," and haven't watched a single program all the way through.

For children, it is doubly hard. They have so many things vying for their attention; they are rarely placed in a position of having to sustain prolonged interest in anything past the time span of a movie. As for time to simply sit and contemplate who they are and where they fit in the world...

It could all get pretty confusing. Especially when you are faced with having to train up your children in those murky areas you don't even have a handle on, yourself. It gets a bit difficult trying to keep to a schedule, keep up with the work and the homework, settle a dozen minor disputes, and still have enough of whatever it takes to make any deposits into your child's future.

Like steer them in some sort of direction, find out where their talents lie, or at least find out what they're doing and thinking when they think you're not watching them. There is nothing worse than commending yourself that nine-year-old Mary, has not argued about going to bed for a week, only to find she has been listening to questionable music on an older sibling's phone under the covers every night. What do you do with a child whose choices are so consistently opposite of yours you are seriously considering not letting her have any more until she grows up? Or, at least gets as big as you.

You maybe could do that when she's nine but the thing could really come back on you by the time she makes it to thirteen. After four years of this kind of relationship, she might end up thinking you don't like her, at all. What's worse is you might not.

What about that six-year-old you promised could pick out her own dress next time and the only one she latches onto is a terrible puke green with an ugly picture of an alien on the front? Certainly there are times when a parent must change her mind or take something back, if for no other reason than to maintain her own sanity. Right?

Which brings us back to the choice thing, again. With the candle burning on both ends, here, because while the child is busy grappling passionately (ever notice how these things are always going down passionately?) the parent is having to make a few choices of her own. Like how important is this thing, anyway? Is it worth a squash to the psyche? Or a reprimand for making a scene? And the big one: what's it going to cost in the long run to just let it go?

The key here is not to take away the choices, but to trade them for several acceptable ones, instead. And don't haggle over what's acceptable. You choose what's acceptable. What you are offering to your children is the opportunity to choose something before you are forced (by their lack of cooperation) to choose for them. As stated before, nine times out of ten, a child will always go for this option because any choice is better than no choice at all. That's human nature.

Acceptable choices are good for everybody. It gives you the wider circle of control without taking the power of choice away from your children. And once again, you have successfully fended off those flaming darts that always seem to be aimed at undermining your relationship. It really is a "no lose" situation because even if you are forced once or twice to walk away without any choice being made in order to break a stalemate (most children will inevitably push the limit at some time or another), you can even go so far as to be sympathetic with their inability to make one this time. This is ultimately still their choice because you took nothing away, and the "response-ability" still rests with them to choose.

> *Acceptable choices are good for everybody.*

It is also good practice for a child to learn that sixty percent of life's choices are not life and death issues. There are many times when the choice they make is not what they would have picked first, or even second. But to make one in any case always promotes judgment and a healthy sense of independence as opposed to a rebellious one.

Following are a few tips to help make "acceptable choices"

work even better for you:

NEVER CRITICIZE A CHOICE, even if it wasn't the one you were hoping for. A choice is very close to an opinion and can easily become a personal offense if put down.

DON'T CHANGE YOUR MIND. If you say it, do it. The repercussions of going back on your word far outweigh a poor choice and could turn into a personal lack of respect for you.

> *Children mirror emotions faster than they feel them.*

TRY NOT TO GET EMOTIONAL. Children mirror emotions faster than they feel them. If you stay calm and rational, they will be less apt to fly off into a tangent, themselves.

NEVER ARGUE ABOUT WHETHER OR NOT YOUR CHOICES ARE ACCEPTABLE. If you allow your children to bargain on this issue, you will soon slip back into letting them call the shots instead of you.

BE POSITIVE. Say something nice about a successful transaction. Show a little appreciation for your children's cooperation. They'll knock themselves out to make choices that please you, just to hear it.

BE FAIR. Acceptable choices must be acceptable all the way around. Taking away the game device or getting an extra chore are not fair choices to trade for listening to unacceptable music. Fifteen minutes to listen to something you approve of, or the promise of a new song purchase, if they give up the old one, will work better. Turning choices into punishments will only backfire and cause you to lose the power that making choices can give.

Everyone needs to feel empowered. To make choices gives us a sense of that power, and to make good ones is the stuff good people are made of. So if you—like the rest of us—are feeling like a great portion of the choices being offered today aren't worth the time to consider, do your kids a favor and cut some of them out.

It's one more way to turn your family time into quality time.

15

The Winner's Circle

Ever since the government loosened its hold on the gambling laws in our country, state lotteries have created a few millionaires and a few million dreamers. An amazing amount of people participate in these activities. And although it is a known fact that only a small percentage of them will actually become winners, every participant not only knows what he would do if he won but has spent considerable time making elaborate plans on just exactly how he would do it. It is not within the nature of every human to take chances. But it is human nature to believe that what happened once, can happen, again. Gambling is based on this.

In fact, it is one of the strongest impulses in human nature. Something the psychologists refer to as the power of "intermittent reward." It has been scientifically proven time and again, that something that pays off every time, does not have as strong an influence as something that only pays off once in a while. And if the stakes are high, the impulse to take a chance on it only intensifies. Everybody wants to be a winner.

The drive to win is the primary reason we play games. This drive is so strong that the human psyche will actually override the more numerous times we lose by allowing us to dream of winning. And this dreaming fuels the fire of our enthusiasm for each new effort. It has nothing to do with age. Once again, we are talking about something that is so integral to human nature that a child is born with this facility fully intact.

> *Everybody wants to be a winner.*

All toddlers seem to enjoy taking things in and out of cupboards. But a toddler who finds a jellybean in a cup on one of these adventures, will not only increase the amount of time spent at the game, he will consistently reach for the cups, first. And if intermittent rewards prove to be golden moments for children, they can be a virtual gold mine for the parent who takes advantage of them.

So, should you reward your children for their propensity to take chances? Not hardly. But a wise parent will always seize the opportunity to utilize a force that is already in operation and channel it—like electricity—into a more purposeful use. To do this, we have to take a closer look at the subject of rewards. So, let's go back to the jellybean.

A child that is given a jellybean every time she picks up her toys will soon assume that it is her rightful due. It is her payment which she has earned for the task. If that is the case, she has every right to opt for not doing it once in a while, especially if she's not in the mood for jellybeans. To up the ante to two jellybeans at this point might get the job done but it is only a temporary fix because your candy is no longer a reward but a bribe. And a bribe is a bribe whether you're talking about jellybeans or the Mafia: eventually it is never enough and almost always leads to a bad end.

This is not to say that allowances or paydays—or anything else that comes regularly for services rendered—will eventually lose its pull. But these are not rewards. They are contracts mutually agreed upon beforehand. Fair earnings. In fact, most people would be insulted if someone referred to what they earned as a reward because a reward implies an inflated value on something you really weren't expecting in the first place. Looking at one's efforts for any length of time in this way eventually results in low self-esteem and lack of respect for others.

That's because truth and fairness are the ultimate highest standards of human nature no matter what culture you come from. To offend these two things at any age in any instance causes immediate breach in relationships that—if not purposefully mended—will remain perpetually torn.

On the other hand, a reward is temporary, uncommon, and sometimes even surprising. Because it never follows a pattern there is an air of mystery about it that automatically catches interest. Humans love a mystery. To say, "Why, Sarah, you picked up your toys without even being asked—what a surprise! I think maybe this calls for a jellybean," has more pull than the actual jellybean. Simply because it was an unexpected surprise... and something of a mystery as to why you came up with it at this particular time.

And don't worry if tomorrow she runs up excitedly and says, "I picked up my toys, again, can I have a jellybean?" Because then you are in a wonderful position to say, "Getting a jellybean every time you pick up your toys would be a lot of jellybeans! But you know what? Picking up toys is a lot of work and if you're willing to work that hard, then I'm willing to pay you for it. As long as you think a jellybean is fair."

All right, you say. So much for Sarah. But suppose you have fathered a walking tornado who would never dream of picking up his own toys, much less, cooperate with any efforts to set up the routine. That's when your experience as an adult wins out over the child. You "set him up" to win. If lotteries can cater to a greater audience than would ever—by nature—frequent casinos, simply by selling the idea, we ought to at least be able to do that much with mere children.

And we can.

You know what makes your little tornado tick better than anyone in the world, for the mere fact that you were probably a tornado, yourself, at that age. So, dig back into those resources and remind yourself what appeals the most. Then set him up to win. "Catch him doing good." Even if you have to go so far as to reward him for not making as big a mess as he did yesterday… that's a starting point. The beginning of the road. And if you can find the road, you can make the journey.

Remember, no one has a greater influence over children, for good or for bad, than their parents. So, don't take surface reactions for the deep stuff. The truth is, any reward coming from you is doubly potent, simply because it comes from you. In the long run, they will knock themselves out to please you. You might not see the effects of it today or tomorrow, or maybe even next week. But you'll see it. So plain it will be like looking into a mirror someday. Which is a pretty high complement to you.

By setting your children up for rewards, and then rewarding them for doing good, you can condition them to win. The determination to win is one of the most wonderful advantages you could ever give your children in life. It would actually have a boomerang effect and make you successful. And who knows? You could be nurturing an Einstein, or an Edison, or—as we Americans are fond of saying, "the next president of the United States."

Here are a few tips that make for good rewards:

Pick something that they already do well, and **GIVE THEM AN UNEXPECTED REWARD** for it.

MAKE THE CHALLENGES ATTAINABLE. The promise of something special for getting an "A" in science, is not a reward, it's a goal. An unexpected activity or treat for doing a good job on a specific assignment or project in science is.

ALWAYS FOLLOW THROUGH. If you promise a movie for something well done, don't come up with some excuse why you can't do it when Saturday comes around. Your word is as good as a promise in your child's eyes, so if you say it, do it.

DON'T BASE YOUR REWARDS SOLELY ON PERFORMANCE. Sometimes a simple, "I like your smile, today, let's do something fun together," can have amazing effects. It means your acceptance of them stretches past what they do to who they are... and that's worth a million.

NEVER ATTACH STRINGS TO YOUR REWARDS. If you reward them for something one day, and they totally bomb out with it the next, don't punish them for it, or take away the reward you gave them yesterday. A reward is like a seed in the ground with the potential to spring up later into something wonderful. Snatch it back and there's no potential for growth, at all.

DON'T OVERDO IT! Rewards are like dessert: too much loses impact and could even make you sick. Remember, the secret here is "intermittent."

It's a wonderful thing to get a turn in the winner's circle. Letting your children experience this in your home will not only be a benefit to their home-life, it could very well be a benefit to their future. Most winners aren't born, they're made. So, make a difference in your children's experiences by "setting them up." And when you do…

Set them up to win.

The Program

16

Phase One

Changing behavior is a necessary part of parenting, especially in this modern era when so much of a child's time is spent with other people. In the old days, our worlds were smaller. It wasn't as difficult to notice if a child "got up on the wrong side of the bed," or to correct some minor infraction that was taking place under a parent's eye. But these days, parents are most likely to have their eyes in other places unless there is a problem.

It is also true that teachers and daycare workers are reluctant to point out every little infraction, simply because it is more reasonable (for everybody involved) to take care of discipline themselves unless a problem persists. By that time the unwanted behavior is fairly well ingrained in the child's habits and takes more than a 'talking to" to get rid of. If ever. Another ingredient to this dilemma is a parent's avoidance of confrontations in the already limited span allotted to spend with their children.

Morning and bedtime routines, by their very nature, are usually consistent enough to produce a false sense of well-being because the activities and participants are the same every day. These brief periods do not allow parents to observe how their child responds to an authority other than themselves, or how they interact with others. All too often, it is an unscheduled parent conference or a dreaded "N" (needs improvement) on a report card that gives an unsuspecting parent the first clue that their little darling has been carrying on an unacceptable behavior for months.

Sadly, what usually ensues is a bitter cycle of groundings or similar punishments that tend to increase negative behavior at alarming rates rather than produce the desired results. Which brings about frustrations on both sides that often lead to resentments and bitter disputes in what was once a fairly peaceful home. On top of that, our current trend to relegate every outlandish behavior to a normal quest for independence on the child's part sometimes tempts parents not to deal with the issue at all. Instead, they hope that it is simply a phase they will one day grow out of.

If Sally does not share her toys in preschool, there is every possibility that the problem will slip by until she is fourteen. At which point a parent may be shocked by her being attracted to "the wrong crowd," or possessing a self-image that Mom and Dad cannot believe would be so low after they have loved her so much all these years. On the other hand, if Billy is a biter, this will get immediate attention from everybody, and the unwanted behavior will be squashed like an intruding insect. This is proven by the fact that the only biters to be found in the adult world are vampires... which is a different problem altogether.

Behavior affects the quality of life. Good behavior makes life better and bad behavior makes life worse. Plain and simple. And the child who learns this early will be ahead of the child who doesn't. The more parents can help their children learn good behaviors, the easier will be their adjustments and understanding in the great wide world ahead of them. Which is why nearly every parent comes to a point at some time or other when it becomes necessary to change a child's behavior. There are many methods for changing unwanted behaviors. This particular one is geared to the natural impulses of human nature. Why? Because utilizing drives that are already in motion simply makes the job easier.

The first step to changing any behavior is to start small.

If Johnny is having trouble paying attention at school, the first thing he needs is a reason to change. Other than an irate parent telling him to "Straighten up when the teacher's talking, do you hear me? I don't want to get note like this, again!" Equally doomed is a response like, "If you can go all week without getting in trouble, I'll..." A week is huge. It isn't even today; it's floating off somewhere in the future. Between now and a week there are a thousand tantalizing temptations to avoid. Like sitting next to a best friend. Or discovering a hangnail. Or, the biggest temptation of them all: someone else talks first. The world outside of one's home is a very exciting and distracting place and our public schools have become boring by comparison. The only thing that comes close to weighing in as an equal is a reward.

At this point, mere praise from an appreciative parent is not enough. Nor is the promise of a treat or something special at the end of the day if he makes it through all the way without failing his mission. The unwanted behavior is already a habit pattern and habits do not have to pass through the thinking process before being engaged... they just happen.

The secret here is not to start with the impulse that is already set, but with the child's own thinking process, which is the only thing strong enough to change the impulse. CAUTION: dealing with the thinking process does not mean giving a lecture on why it is important to behave in class. That is quite irrelevant at the moment because it is obviously not important to Johnny. But a good parent can make it important.

Here's how:

> **CHOOSE AN APPEALING REWARD**. You know your child and the things or activities that are most appealing. It doesn't have to be something purchased—children are always enthusiastic about activities, especially if it includes some one-on-one time.

> **MAKE A REACHABLE GOAL**. For example, if Johnny's first session of the day is math, send a note to be signed by the teacher if he can successfully make it through the lesson without being disruptive (approximately half an hour). Don't go "note crazy" and start dividing the day up into half-hour increments Remember, we're starting small. We are dealing with one session, for one time period only.

> **DO NOT BE NEGATIVE IF THE GOAL IS NOT REACHED THE FIRST DAY**. Now is the time for a discussion but not on the importance of listening in

class. The topic should be an acknowledgement of the difficulty of that task, and ideas on how he might succeed tomorrow. For instance, if sitting next to a best friend is making it impossible for Johnny not to talk during the math lesson, he might try requesting to sit somewhere else for that half hour. Not "for good," though. The thought of not sitting next to a best friend FOREVER is too much of a shock, but a half hour (in his mind), he maybe could handle.

> *If you say it, do it*

NEVER TAKE AN EARNED REWARD AWAY. If Johnny did wonders in math that first day but behaved totally outrageous in the afternoon science lesson, think of some other way to handle it that has nothing to do with the reward he already earned. And give it gladly. To make a deal and then not follow through for any reason will lower the respect your child has for you. If you say it, do it.

DON'T QUIT TOO SOON. Remember, it takes two weeks to create a habit. The goal should be to make it through two weeks without fail. If a day or two goes by when he doesn't make it through, you start over. When he successfully completes the two weeks, you can then relegate behavior in math class to "Phase Two" of the reward program.

DON'T OVERLOAD THE CIRCUITS. The temptation to add another session or behavior pattern to work on grows stronger the closer Johnny gets to his goal. But don't do it. Added pressures and unexpected failures at this time tend to be taken very personally and have repercussions in the self-image department While Johnny is working on his goal, the major goal of his parents must be to make sure he succeeds.

SHOW YOUR ENCOURAGEMENT. Lavish on the praise when he succeeds. Avoid phrases like, "That's how you should have been acting in the first place." And never begrudge the reward. If you made a bargain to stop at the local mini-mart for a treat every day he succeeds, or play a half hour of his favorite game before bed... do it with enthusiasm. Even if you're sick and tired of whatever it is, or hadn't realized how it would break into the time you normally spent doing something else, stay positive for the fact that he is successfully changing his behavior. Realize that if it's been an effort or drudgery for you, his part has been equally—or more so—for him.

The secret to being successful with "Phase One" of changing behavior is to start small, give frequent attainable rewards, and to be consistent enough to form new habits. The time it takes to form good habits is time well spent, even when starting out small. That's because once the training process shifts over into habit, it never has to be "relearned" again. It then frees up the thinking process for going on to other things.

Like "Phase Two."

17

Phase Two

The goal of any reward system is to ultimately be replaced by a desired behavior. It is a law of Nature. The human psyche works in this way, and—like many of the other principles we have talked about—works both negatively and positively. The same as electricity. One of the most vivid examples of this is the drug dealer who is commonly known to give out the first of his merchandise for free. Then for a minimal fee. Then for any high price he desires. Why does this work so well?

Because the desired behavior has already become a habit.

Any behavior, no matter how "ingrained," can be counteracted by a reward that is equal or above its value. Even though it is only the child's own desire that can change a behavior, parents hold the power over their children to change those desires. In the example of Johnny not being able to listen in class, the behavior was changed by starting small, making achievable goals, and being consistent. There was only one goal for "Phase One": a successful two-week run of the desired behavior.

At this point, many parents think the job is done and go to work on another problem spot without ever having gone on to "Phase Two." Consequently, when the original unwanted behavior pops up again (seemingly out of nowhere), it is extremely frustrating for both parent and child. One rarely goes back to the original reward routine for correcting it because everyone thinks they tried that, already, and it obviously didn't work. But that is the very time when it is most important to go back—because your foundation for change is already laid.

It will not only be easier the second time, it will be doubly powerful. Why? Because while you were busy working with the physical problem of Johnny not listening in class, something was subconsciously changed in his thinking process that will help you, later. With many more behaviors than just listening in class.

"Phase One" is limited. It has merely succeeded in raising a wall. But without reinforcements, even a beautiful wall is unable to stand up to the pressure of daily living. The same is true of human behavior. We are building a unique (and hopefully wonderful) human being as we raise our children, and—like any other piece of construction that must withstand the elements of life—it must be built strong enough to withstand whatever use it is put to.

Since it is human nature to relegate what is already mastered to that part of the brain which takes no thought to the "hows and whys" anymore, it should come as no surprise that the child will lose interest in what is no longer a challenge. But if the desired behavior is still not set in cement, what do you do?

It's time to up the ante.

Like the drug dealer who begins to charge a small fee, you increase the value of the desired behavior by increasing the reward. With one small catch: it takes longer than a day to earn. It takes a week. Before Phase One that request would have been unbelievable for the child, and he might not have even wanted to try. But he has already done successfully what you are asking him to do. He has done more than a week, he has actually made it through two. He knows it is possible, but the big question is, does he want to? That's why it's time to change the reward.

Don't give in to the temptation to cheat here. Children are not dumbbells. The promise of a fantastic vacation when you have every intention of taking one anyway, is not fair. The child is putting forth tremendous effort, even if you think this kind of behavior should come through some kind of osmosis and he should do it naturally. He is setting up patterns for life and it is your opinion of the value of those patterns that will determine his. If the only reason you are doing all this is to avoid another embarrassing confrontation with the school, then…

Don't worry. Stick to the steps and it will work for you anyway. What's more, your child will get a lot more out of it than you will in the long run. Here are the steps for Phase Two.

STAY AHEAD OF YOUR CHILD with the program. Don't wait until he becomes board with the daily routine (or the rewards) to change over to Phase Two. The first time he makes it through a successful two weeks, kick things into high gear and keep him charged. For instance, if you have given him fifty cents a day for a reward, tell him how impressed you are with his achievement and that it was worth every penny to you. So much that you would even be willing to give him, say... five dollars on Saturday, instead of fifty cents every day.

STAY AGE APPROPRIATE. For the sake of example, we have been using Johnny, who is having problems listening in grade school. If you have a high school student who is having the same problem, an activity with a parent after school, or fifty cents a day, is not going to cut it. Extra phone privileges or time with friends are more valuable rewards for an older child.

BE ENCOURAGING. Though the rewards are physical, there is an opportunity here to develop "response ability" in your child. Give praise and recognition for success at every opportunity and avoid the temptation to put down failures. Instead, be sympathetic and encourage him that tomorrow is a brand new day and he can start over. Express your faith in him that he can do it. Pretty soon, it will be your words he seeks after more than the rewards.

> *All behaviour takes practice.*

DON'T BE DISCOURAGED if it takes longer then you think to get to Phase Two. All behavior takes practice. Chances are, it took a lot more than a few weeks for the unwanted habits to develop in the first place.

BE CONSISTENT. Once again, consistency is your best ally in changing behavior. While you are busy with your program, the mere repetition of it is busy reinforcing the pattern in the child's subconscious. And if you think you've seen this tip crop up on more than one list in this book, you're absolutely right. For obvious reasons.

BE PATIENT. Almost everything of value in Life takes time and the time you invest in your children will pay far better dividends than the pastimes you traded them for.

STAY REASONABLE. Don't go overboard with the rewards. Put some time and thought into what you will agree to before you commit because your honor is on the line.

Phase Two of changing behavior is an often overlooked step in the reward system. Yet, in the same way that setting the hook is a reasonable guarantee that your fish won't get away, stretching out the time span between rewards takes a surface relationship with a behavior to a deeper level. It turns it into a habit. And good habits make children that behave better. Which in turn makes happier parents. Now the question is, "What next?" Is there a Phase Three?

You bet.

18

Phase Three

We have looked at rewards as the most efficient system for changing behavior. In Phase One we saw how the rewards needed to be frequent and equal to the value of effort necessary to make the change. In Phase Two we discussed the necessity of lengthening the time between those rewards, and of maintaining interest levels by raising reward values during that time. But as mentioned before, the ultimate goal of any reward system is to produce a desired behavior that will carry on indefinitely without the rewards. So, even though one might be proceeding along quite nicely in the desired goals, they are still in a temporary position.

Phase Three takes the final step of exchanging rewards for reinforcements. To do this, we begin by finding a suitable medium of exchange. At this point, you should have a few things already in place that have been subconsciously at work for you. The first is praise. If you have been lavishing on the praise at every opportunity, your approval rating should have increased sufficiently in your child's eyes to hold some swaying power of its own by now.

You can measure this power by the response your child has to your words of encouragement. Does their face light up? Do they suddenly strive even harder to please you? Do you see them imitating your praise techniques to siblings or friends as a part of their own interaction with others? If not, you either haven't been frequent enough with your praise, or you haven't been demonstrative enough. Simply make an adjustment to your deliveries, and your children will respond in the above ways. Guaranteed.

Because it is human nature.

If it doesn't happen instantly, it's only because it is out of character for you and will take a little time to surpass your child's disbelief that such communication is really happening between you. If you're "just not the praising type"... then change your type. Changing behavior works for adults as well as children, and this kind of communication between parent and child offers rewards that go way beyond childhood.

> *Changing behavior works for adults as well as children*

The second thing working for you is the child's own success in the thing you are asking him to do. By the time you reach Phase Three there should no longer be any question in the child's mind whether or not he is capable of achieving this goal. At this point, he has already done it. That isn't to say the behavior is written in stone, just yet, but the cement is definitely drying. Both you and the child have discovered that the behavior is sustainable.

* But for how long?

The Nature Of Children

* And in the child's eyes, "What's the point?"

* Now is the time to introduce the powerhouse of behavior modification: the point system.

Points work for everybody. In the real world as well as the world of childhood. Points are the next best medium of exchange to money. If you find this hard to believe, just look at the stock exchange, the measurement for bank loans, or insurance tables. Points, in their many forms, are a necessary part of modern living. When your child graduates to a point system for desired behavior he is already taking a vital step into the real world. He's forming good life habits... which make life good.

When it comes to point systems, age doesn't matter. If you have a toddler that is learning to share, points will work. If you have a teenager who wants driving time in the family car, points will work. If you have a child who spends way too much time on video games instead of interacting with others, points will work. The only difference between all these scenarios is the trade-in value that the points stand for. Customize what the points stand for to your own family needs and values. Once again, consistency is t the main key, here. For constant behavior you need constant reinforcements.

That doesn't mean you have to forever be rewarding Johnny for listening in class, from the third grade when you began until high school graduation. It means you have to get him in the habit of exchange. That's the purpose of Phase Three. When we successfully exchange rewards for points, then we can successfully exchange the rewards and reinforcements for other behaviors. Move on to something else you want to work

> *When it comes to point systems, age doesn't matter.*

on. That's changing behavior in a nutshell. That's using the secrets of human nature to achieve your success.

So, let's look a little closer at point systems. Here are the necessary ingredients:

EACH POINT MUST HAVE A SPECIFIC VALUE. If ten points is worth an ice cream at the local ice cream shop on one week, it can't be exchanged without notice (and agreement from both parties) to a dish out of the freezer of whatever is left in there. No substitutes without going back to the bargaining table.

THE YOUNGER THE CHILD, THE MORE VISUAL THE SYSTEM. Colorful charts, stickers, and animated praise from parents, works best with the little ones. Put the chart on the refrigerator (or some other visual location). Use colored markers, drawings, and—if you're not artistic—there are numerous commercial items like this already out there in the marketplace. Charts for household chores and bedtime habits like brushing teeth... the point is to put up something tangible. Young children are "concrete." They need to see it, feel it, and touch it. And what is animated praise? Instead of saying, "Good job, Jennifer, Dad's proud of you," you say, "Way to go, Jenny!" (raised voice, big smile, here. Clap, hug, even jump up and down if you can find it in your psyche to do so. If not, give it your best shot). Remember, it isn't praise unless the child knows it is.

MAKE POINTS REDEEMABLE AT SPECIFIC TIMES.

One of the most common pitfalls of the point system is to let it dwindle away during the business of daily living, and suddenly it's been weeks since you've had a redemption session. Start from the beginning to set a certain time for redeeming those points. No longer than once a week for younger children. The older ones can go a bit longer for something more valuable, such as a special dress for the prom, or a coveted event that's coming up. But make sure these occasions are never overlooked or it is your reputation that will suffer.

NEVER TAKE POINTS AWAY. Your paycheck might be "all spent" when you finally get it, but you'd get pretty disgusted if an employer took money out beforehand for something you didn't do just right last week. So do kids. Points earned are points earned. They're sacred. Never take them back for bad behavior, even if you have a junior Machiavellian on your hands. There are other ways to deal with unacceptable behavior.

DO NOT TAKE ACHIEVEMENTS LIGHTLY. Never make light of something your child has put a tremendous amount of effort into. Just because you assume everyone should be able to wake up enough to use the bathroom at night, don't belittle your child's efforts (or failures) to do so. Always remember that, whether it's verbalized or not, it is your approval that is ultimately the most important reason for your child's desire to work toward anything, and that's a big responsibility.

DON'T LET INTEREST LAG. If success doesn't happen fast enough, or if it comes too fast, readjust the system. The best point systems need to stay fine-tuned to the specific and particular needs of the child. If you know from experience that Sally is worthless for much of anything after eight o'clock, that's no time to schedule a family conference to discuss point values. In the same way, if Jimmy has been trying unsuccessfully for three days not to have physical confrontations with his brother, you need to readjust the value of the points so that they reflect a greater incentive for him to try harder. Similarly, if the learned behavior has become common place or too easy, it's time to go on to the next phase. Or the next challenge altogether.

HAVE A "GRAND FINALE." There must always be an end to every quest, a holy grail to discover, or at the very least, a prize to be won. Choose a grand goal for that final achievement and carry it out with a little fanfare to signify a satisfying end. Make a big deal out of it and then it is finished. But as with the rewards themselves, make the end justify the means. One need not have a trip to Europe to celebrate potty training.

DON'T WAIT UNTIL SOMETHING IS WRONG TO INSTIGATE ANOTHER POINT SYSTEM. Everyone should always be working on something. If there's no problem area to work on at the moment, pick a goal to achieve (like learning a new skill) that is approached in the same manner. This will not only keep the control systems in place, it will make a habit of the practice of continually bettering yourself. That's the way high achievers are made.

Changing behavior is at the same time both simple and complex. Half the secret of success in this endeavor is to understand the reasons for the behavior in the first place. The truth is, there is no easy solution to any behavioral problem. Understanding human nature and utilizing the forces that are already in motion in the psyche of a child, simply makes it easier. It still takes a tremendous amount of effort on not only your part as a parent, but on your child's part as a child. All children go through phases. Wouldn't it be nice to have more of a say in which ones they went through?

You can.

Part Three:

Training Up

Raising The Standard

19. In Training
20. Living with an Attitude
21. Making Problems
22. Common Ground
23. The Meaning of Things

The Pursuit of Excellence

24. A Matter of Taste
25. Doing What's Best
26. Doing Things on Purpose
27. About Time
28. The Search for Together

Raising The Standard

19

In Training

All children are in training. Whether they have a specific program, a good coach or a bad one, children are driven from within to practice newfound skills. It's part of their nature. Over the years, there has been great controversy on the best ways to do this. Some have even gone so far as to proclaim that the best way is to have no way at all, and to simply let the children ferret out their own ways.

But even ferrets train up their young. Passing along secrets in the world of Nature is a survival thing and failure to master certain skills can be the deciding factor as to whether an animal lives out its life to the fullest or dies young. In the same way, many of History's successful families have remained so for generations—not because they had a corner on producing more than their share of offspring with high IQ—but because they passed the secrets of success down to their children.

If children learn sixty percent by watching, thirty percent by doing and only ten percent by what is told to them, maybe we should be a little more concerned about what they see. And if you are thinking what you fail to teach your child at home will be covered in school, think, again. Everything after the fifth grade is nothing but review, except for a few subjects like algebra and biology, which are merely requirements for higher education.

In the present public system it has become more important to learn how to operate a computer or drive a car than to teach the value and maintenance of human relationships. So, until they start offering Dale Carnegie's book *How To Win Friends and Influence People* as a reading requirement for graduation, the job of teaching "Life 101" is pretty much left up to the parent.

In spite of recent trends, there are still only two ways to do this. Training up or training down. There are numerous methods to prove either way but the fact remains that the coin only has two sides and it's going to land "heads" or "tails" no matter how you throw it. Good or bad. Positive or negative. Up or down.

Oddly enough, the most widely accepted method is to train down. Most parents feel that discipline means to keep their children in line or correct them when they do bad things. The trouble is, interaction is pretty limited on this level. It is sporadic, and almost always emotional. In this method the boundaries most often stay on the physical plane, even though — in the long run — the soul turns out to be a much better captain of behavior.

On the other hand, training up has a much wider range of possibilities. A bevy of acceptable choices for challenging achievements is a more potent system of motivation than a list of rules telling us what we cannot do. A parent who motivates by encouragement instead of bossiness, becomes a counselor rather than a dictator. And while it is the destiny of all dictators to eventually be overthrown, the wisdom of good counselors gets passed down from generation to generation.

Training up promotes self-discipline as opposed to enforced boundaries. In the same way a fence is an open challenge to get around, under or through; a ladder is a temptation to climb. And if boredom is a major problem in today's homes, training for something of value provides the interest and time enrichment that idleness denies.

The dictionary defines discipline as "instruction; training of the mind, or body, or the moral faculties; subjection to authority; self-control; (and finally) to improve behavior by judicious penal methods." So, if Webster is following his typical method of listing things in the order of their importance, we should probably begin at the top instead of the bottom of this list.

History proves that successful people are disciplined people and children that experience the benefits of a disciplined life early on, will advance farther and faster than those who don't. Training Up promotes determination and perseverance in an otherwise passive world. It provides an outlet for those frustrating periods of high energy and closed in spaces that so many families today are faced with. But don't confuse training up with sports or hobbies alone.

Unless these things are linked with goal planning and personal

> *In order for an interest to hold, there has to be a reason.*

development, they become nothing more than glorified pastimes. It is human nature to be constantly striving with the status quo and asking, why So, in order for an interest to hold, there has to be a reason. Point out the reasons along Life's roadways. Engaging the mind will hold the attention much longer than merely engaging the body.

To realize that everything in the world has a connection—and then to hunt for those connections—gives children the mental organization for clear thinking. Learning becomes a challenge that turns into confidence with each new discovery. To set goals and achieve them is the best form of personal development there is, and always leads to higher self-esteem.

Johnny will get more out of his piano lessons if he is practicing for a concert than simply learning one song after another. And if he discovers that people actually enjoy his performance, he will develop more than a deeper commitment to his music: he will become hooked on bringing pleasure to others. Anytime a child rises to an occasion, or grasps hold of a value and makes it part of himself, he is being trained up. To make practice times a torture by threatening chores or punishments if not carried out to the letter, is training down.

> *The effort we put into things adds value to them.*

The effort we put into things adds value to them. By nature, children spend the greatest amount of their effort—not on what has become routine—but right out on the very edge of their reach. That's why it's important for us as parents to keep up with them. We must make it a priority not to treat Sarah like a five-year-old if she is six or seven. Not only will it hinder her achievements, it will foster complacency and boredom with her daily routines. It will become more difficult to spark her natural enthusiasms.

The time to let children help in the cooking is when they eager to learn how, even though it's more work for you while they learn. Don't criticize them if more lettuce and tomatoes end up on the floor than in the salad bowl. If you have more patience now, you won't be wondering why they aren't the least bit interested at the age of ten: it's because you've been doing everything for them up until then and they have long since changed interests while you were waiting for them to get bigger. Or at least more coordinated.

Here are some guidelines to help you recognize a "training up" opportunity:

IF THEY ASK, LET THEM TRY. It means their curiosity and enthusiasm are prime for this activity, even if they need some help to accomplish it.

CONVERT NEGATIVES TO POSITIVES. If Billy wants a paper route, don't say, "No, you're too young." Exchange it for something like "I'm sure you're responsible enough. But we'll have to wait until you're a little older before we can talk about it." Or, instead of "If you don't finish cleaning this room, I'm going to…" Try: "You're doing a great job so far! Think you can finish before dinner?" And you can always exchange "Get in this house right now!" to "You can have five more minutes before you have to come in."

ASK THEM WHY. Encourage them to express themselves so they will be comfortable communicating with others.

RAISE THE STANDARD. Training up always encourages to try harder, reach higher, learn more, do more, and say more. It never discourages or puts anybody down.

BE CONSISTENT. If your child sets a goal, help them keep at it. If your teenager is on a diet, change family pizza night to taco salad or broiled dinner once in a while. If they start a project, help them out if they lag toward the finish. "Up the ante" and encourage them to keep on.

LET THE WHOLE FAMILY TAKE PART in encouraging each other's talents. A preschooler's alphabet is just as important as big brother's Little League when families stick together.

TAKE THE OPPOSITE. Instead of condemning children for being selfish, encourage them to share. Instead of noticing something out of place, look for something that's in.

The decision to train up or down rests solely with the parent. However, many times parents are not aware that they have any choice in the matter, at all. That's because most of us will stick to the same method our own parents used when we were children. It's only when we run into trouble that we seem to start looking around for a better way of doing things. But any efforts you make to Train Up your children will come back to you in multiple rewards. Not only will you be turning more family time into quality time, you'll be turning out children of purpose.

So, train them up.

20

Living With an Attitude

Attitudes are contagious. They can be admired or looked down upon at the same time, and for that reason, they are something of a paradox for the modern parent. If aggressive is what we have been calling a "winning" attitude for so long, exactly how much is too much? Because frankly, most of these perpetually aggressive personalities are pretty hard to live with.

Children with "bad attitudes" become the most important person in their lives from a very early age. Not because they are born that way but because they are allowed to be. It is human nature to be aggressive. But our problems with aggression these days, is that we have forgotten just exactly what the word means. So, let's take a closer look at it.

Aggression is like fire, or any other force of nature: without a degree of control, it turns rampantly destructive. Webster's defines the word aggression as: "the practice of making assaults or attacks; offensive action in general." In terms of the word aggressive (which we like to think of more as "decisive in business") it states: "the practice of the invasion of another's rights or territory."

When Jenny will not eat her vegetables because she "hates peas" and mother allows it, two things will happen. First, it teaches Jenny that she is more important than either her mother or the family group. Secondly, it sets mother up for years of bickering over this issue in front of family and friends because she will not always want to cater to it. Especially at times when it gets embarrassing. Similarly, a child who will not give up his favorite chair to a visiting adult when company comes—and his parents let him—will not only grow up into an unpleasant companion, he will one day long to be, and won't know how. Which is one of the saddest forms of neglect a parent can bestow on a child.

If the word neglect seems too strong, let it be stated that the response of our own judicial system to the surprised parents of delinquent children who say, "But I gave her everything she ever wanted!" are promptly informed that they neglected to give her what she needed (a sense of values), and are therefore charged with neglect. But let's look a little closer. Because like all the forces of human nature, there are two sides to every coin.

Aggression is merely determination turned backward.

> Aggression is merely determination turned backward.

According to *Webster's*, determination is: "the act of coming to a decision or of resolving something." In reference to being determined, it states: "to be resolute, unwavering, and settled." Both of these characteristics—aggression and determination—take great strength of character. But which one would you, as a parent, rather see instilled in your children? Which one of these traits do you feel would be better for them in the long run? Determination, of course. Why? Because one is pleasant to be around and admirable to look up to. The other is not.

Once again, we have come back to the subject of negative and positive. If you ever recognize the choice between these two things in your parenting, choose positive; if for no other reason than you can rely on the absolute guarantee that nothing bad can come out of it. The negative road sports more hazards than anyone would care to look at. It can be argued that many children survive growing up on the negative road. But so do alligators. Which would you rather live with for eighteen years?

Gone are the days when every sprout was raised with the admonition of, "Why, if you work hard enough, you could be president someday." Now, we feel a measure of success if they simply make it through high school unscathed. There is no debate whether it is a different world today than it was fifty years ago, but human beings are the same. Which is the point and purpose of this book.

As stated from the very beginning, a better understanding of basic human nature can help you change the time you are already spending with your children into quality time. Which in turn can make life better for you and your children. It can even add more quality. And quality is premium.

Only what do you do if you are halfway through your child-rearing days and you've already got a household of alligators? Don't worry. In the same way that it is the nature of the reptile to burst forth from the egg and make a mad fighting dash toward survival, it is the nature of children to respond to their parents.

If they have become alligators, it's only because you have let them. They will be just as determined to "march to your drum" if you start leading them in another direction.

> *It is the nature of children to respond to their parents.*

Following are seven steps toward "flipping that coin" over from aggression to determination.

INSIST ON SHARING. Sharing breeds tolerance, which leads to respect... which is the fundamental positive foundation for all relationships.

INSIST ON COMMON COURTESIES. Being polite promotes self-control, which hones a person's "ability to respond" to others... which leads to being responsible: a trait that is not only profitable within the family, but in society, too.

ENCOURAGE COMMUNICATION AND DEBATE as a means to resolve differences, as opposed to physical force. Should this fail, expound on the privilege to withdraw. Above all, make it perfectly clear that physical confrontations inflict losses on both parties. They should not only be engaged in as an ultimate last resort, but gone into with the full knowledge that there will be consequences to shoulder because of it.

NEVER REMOVE CONSEQUENCES OUT OF SYMPATHY. Having a "hard day" is not an acceptable excuse for bad behavior. You can share sympathy with your children at having to face consequences, and even help field off the pitfalls of having it happen again before the night is over by staying a few steps ahead of them. Don't let them get too tired, too hungry, too bored, or too frustrated without some intervention beforehand instead of after. Dinner going to be late? Set out acceptable snacks. Got a child that gets wound up when they get exhausted? Give them a warm bath. Kids starting to bicker? Give them something acceptable to do (something different than watching the same video they've already seen five times). And if you ever notice frustration levels going over the brink... reach out and lend a hand.

MAKE ANGER UNACCEPTABLE. If you treat anger for what it is—bad behavior—and dole out appropriate consequences for it, you will not have to put up with it being a constant member of your household. Allowing anger to be a reason for violence is criminal: which is one of the ways criminals are made.

DON'T ALLOW BAD LANGUAGE. This doesn't just refer to swearing. An outburst of, "I hate you!" should always be met with, "You're not allowed to hate in this family. You don't have to like the way people behave, or even put up with them, but we will not hate." If this sounds drastic, remember that children will naturally adhere to wherever their parents draw the bottom line. So, if yours has slipped a little too low, lately... lift it up.

CHOOSE HAPPY. Happiness is a choice, not a feeling. If you allow your children to be grumpy or grouchy with you or each other, it can ruin the atmosphere of the entire home. To insist that children be nice, be fair, and be happy is not hard for them. It is a relief. What's more, because they are children, they are amazingly good at it. Unlike adults who are constantly nagged by thoughts of money, work, and the state of the Nation, children can—and should be—oblivious to those things. They also possess that enduring quality of being able to take your mind off those things, too, when you see them being nice, fair, and happy with each other.

If you find yourself having to say, "You better change your attitude!" way too much at your house, it's time to make sure that everybody in the family understands just exactly what an attitude is. Attitude is not a state of being it is a state of mind. And the marvelous thing about a child's mind is that a parent can—and should be—in charge of it. The human brain has an amazing capacity to change behavior by choice. It is this power of choice that sets us apart from the animal world.

Attitudes are a part of life that everyone has to live with. But they are also a reflection of our individual choices. If the old adage that "one bad apple can spoil the whole barrel" is true, it is also true that a single flashlight can lead you through a forest of trees on a dark night. As horrible as a bad attitude can be, a wonderful one is an absolute wonder to be around. It can make a bright spot in any home. And what's even better... it's catching.

No matter how old you are.

21

Making Problems

Many children long for the time when they will be grown up enough not to have to follow their parent's rules. Bedtimes, bath-times, and other such interferences in their day—especially when there are so many other things to choose from—cannot only be inconvenient but cause problems, too.

Problems with their parents who are always enforcing such rules, problems having to explain to their friends why they can or cannot participate in something, and problems with siblings who are constantly on hand to taunt, judge, or actually take their place in the very activity they were called away from. Many wishes go up every day from these young members of society, for a world where there are no rules at all.

Every child knows at least one person who does not have to live with rules. A friend or acquaintance who does not have to scamper home at the first sign of approaching dark, who has enough change in a pocket to visit the nearest mini-mart whenever hunger strikes, and can stay up *all night long* watching movies if they feel like it. They have even been known to wear the very same clothing to school the next day, simply because they are more comfortable than clean ones.

Everybody knows that. And almost every child, by the time they are ten, has heard or even expressed that famous saying which states, "Rules were made to be broken." Maybe even taken great pleasure in it. Which in a parent's dictionary, elevates an opinion to the rank of "an attitude," which in turn becomes something to be dealt with... and dealt with... and dealt with.

Breaking rules is a cycle rampant with so many little successes and failures that it has been relegated to the "normal bin" of daily living. There are many ways of dealing with it, ranging from ignoring it entirely, to literally blasting it out of the home with a barrage of more defensive rules. Rules like: no arguing, no talking back, and a myriad of groundings or punishments for not doing what one is told to do. And everything in between. It is the parent's choice.

> *The quality of life is raised substantially when it goes beyond the survival level.*

Just as surely as it is a parent's right to choose how they will raise their children, it is also just as sure that the parent will eventually be paid out in the consequences of that choice. Children are adaptable, amazingly resilient, and have been known to survive all of the above. But it is also true that the quality of life is raised substantially when it goes beyond the survival level.

The best way to deal with the "war on rules" attitude is to tell the truth.

And the truth about rules is: there is no such thing as growing out of them. Ever. As a person gets older they simply exchange one set of rules for another. Such as, "If you don't work, you don't get paid." Plain and simple. Ninety percent of the adult world abides by this rule with no questions asked. Yet, it is amazing how many of these same parents lead their children to believe otherwise.

A child's protest of, "When I grow up, I'm never going to—" is often met with a response of, "That's fine, but until you do, you are still going to do what I tell you." Of course the parent knows quite well that when their child grows up, there will be no problem with bathing or going to bed when tired. But this part of the conversation is rarely—if ever—discussed.

Nature has arranged things so that most adults are quite capable of either coercing or physically forcing children to follow rules. By the time they are big enough to be any formidable opposition, they have usually been won over. This is proven by the fact that very few adults continue to struggle with childhood rules. On the other hand, an alarming number of adults do continue to struggle with rules. And this is proven not only by the rising rate of crime throughout the world but also in the rising number of traffic fines, bank penalties, and unemployment percentages.

In looking at this dilemma through the eyes of a parent, it becomes imperative to realize that it is not the rules themselves that need to be instilled in children, but their attitude toward those rules. So, in order to better equip our children for a more successful adulthood, we need to give them the whole truth about the way things work. We can do this by broadening their knowledge about *truth* and *consequences*.

Here are some good ways to do that:

HELP YOUR CHILD TO LOOK AT RULES DIFFERENTLY. They are gates and not fences across the road of life. Working with them lets you through, and allows you the freedom to travel on to better things. Refuse to cooperate with that gate and it becomes merely another part of a much larger fence. Sadly, it is possible to live an entire lifetime between two gates on that road, because—as in all things—the ultimate choice still rests with the individual.

DON'T CONFUSE THE ISSUES. Too many rules can have the same effect on children as too many laws have on adults. Speed traps, exorbitant service charges, or unfair tax and legal fees have been known to cause people to avoid living in certain areas and seek out others that are easier to get along with. This is also true of families.

ENCOURAGE POSITIVE ATTITUDES. Most rules have a purpose and some sort of beneficial value to either the individual or the group. To participate in them willingly or even cheerfully makes life more enjoyable for everybody. It even takes less time.

LET YOUR CHILDREN PARTICIPATE in rule making. Whenever you can give them the opportunity to have a vote or a say in something, give it to them. It will result in a sense of worth and responsibility that cannot be achieved with mere words. **Reminder**: This does not mean they are ready to fly the space shuttle. Which is the sort of suggestion you might get if your offer is too vague. Remember to offer *acceptable choices* such as: "Should we have bedtime at eight o'clock, so there is time for a story, or eight-thirty so that you can watch your TV show? But you would have to go right to bed without a story if you did that."

DON'T RESCUE your children from the consequences of breaking rules, or they will not respect the rules. What's more, they will get gratification at having "beat the system" and that sense of power and accomplishment will be stronger than the "sufferings" of the few times they get caught on other occasions. What's more, you will be raising up an expert arguer whose goal is to figure out best how to wear you down and get their own way, which can be discouraging for a tired, work-worn parent to deal with all the time.

DON'T CHANGE THE RULES. True, rules change with the passage of time and accomplishment, and that's the natural progression of things. But if bickering between siblings is not tolerated one night and then overlooked the next... guess which will happen most frequently at your house?

FOLLOW YOUR OWN RULES. Don't expect your children to have enough integrity to stick to rules if you don't show respect for them yourself. Do you speed when there are no policemen around? Do you feel you've come into some luck when the grocery store gives the wrong change? Then your children will be like that, too, because that's human nature.

There really is no such thing as living without rules because life, itself, has rules. The child who can stay out as late as she wants will spend the rest of her life searching for someone who will care enough to worry about her. The boy who sleeps in class because he stayed up all night will not only have difficulties holding down a job later on, he will be limited in the jobs he can choose from because of his lack of education. Those people who do not wash or sufficiently groom themselves, will be shunned by peers. True, life is choices. The whole truth? We must all live with the consequences—or results—of our choices.

There are many successful people in life who give little if no thought to rules. It is not because they have found a way to be free of them. Instead, they have accepted them as a necessary part of living and have adjusted their lives accordingly. Amazingly, this has given them a greater freedom. They are free of those who enforce the law and all of the consequences of those who break it. And they can go farther and do more in life because of this.

> *Rules are a problem only for those who cannot rule themselves.*

If you can teach your children that rules are a problem only for those who cannot rule themselves, then you will not only have a more peaceful home-life today, your children will have a more successful future tomorrow. Show them how to "open those gates" instead of banging their heads against them, and you will be helping them to make progress along that road of life instead of making more problems for them later on.

Common Ground

In a day when the world's values seem to be as diverse as its cultures, parents are spending a lot of time searching for a set of standards that will not only suit their individual philosophies but actually fit in with the way they really live. The official rating system used by the movie and television industry is a good example of this.

While a minor may not attend an "R" rated movie without a parent, the same features are eventually relegated to cable TV where they can be seen, often during prime time, by anyone. Similarly, parents who do not allow their young children to view horror films have virtually no control over the previews of those films that are scattered relentlessly throughout the day without restrictions to time or channels.

It would be nice to say that parents who are really concerned with these issues have the option to supervise their children to the point that the television is only turned on during approved programs, the mute button is effectively used during commercials, and they provide some visual distraction during those commercials that will insure that their darlings are not suffering unwanted assaults on their senses. But how many of us really do that?

In all honesty, supervision in today's homes invariably means that the parents are busy in the kitchen or at the computer while children are occupying themselves at their own discretion for... however long they are quiet. That's because one of the few things that has not changed down through the eons of family history is the belief that "silence is golden."

Especially after a hard and hectic day at the office.

There are a lot of these discrepancies in the lives of today's families. The public schools set certain standards for education and behavior but it is still ultimately the parent who makes the final decision to uphold them, or not. Does everyone enforce the suggested twenty to forty minutes per subject for homework every evening? Hardly. Any child who gets their homework done (in most families) is done. Good enough. A great percentage of children actually get through school by only doing a minimal amount of homework, if any. What they don't get done before and between classes is invariably made up in passing test grades.

The same practices hold true with nutrition. Research has proven that a balanced diet supplemented by vitamins can have noticeable effects on a child's performance in school, as well as their propensity to fend off colds and the flu. But how many families indulge in fast foods (pizza included in this category) at least twice a week, or more. It is not a realistic assessment if you do not include breakfasts and lunches in this survey.

Time is the premium commodity that overrides sound

judgment in this area. Hard working parents not only lack the time to rustle up fresh foods from scratch, it is frequently more expensive to do so. Besides that, children have a tendency to argue about such items as broccoli, carrots, and fresh salads, over a quick stop for a hamburger and fries. And how can you insist that your children substitute milk or water for their beverage during these outings, when you yourself would order a soda, too, because that's what goes best with such fare.

The truth is, quite a few generations have been raised up with these eating habits, and the human race still continues to propagate. What's more, the body is such an amazing and resilient mechanism, that it is possible in most cases to recover optimum health by changing diet and exercise habits in later years. At which time it becomes an individual's personal choice. So, is it really worth the hassle when raising and dealing with children?

Considering the same holds true with almost every standard in our society, are any of them really worth it? If—barring violence, theft, and all manner of perversion—a child can be raised to adulthood with a minimum amount of enforced control, what's the point? The point is, some things make life better.

And some don't.

That's why it is important to use "standard measures" when deciding what you will or will not apply to your family's list of values. Because in spite of the fact that we have never had so much help available in both resources and information for raising up children, we still only have twenty-four hours in a day to do it in. Which means that no normal person can physically (much less mentally) incorporate everything available for this task into their lives. Choices have to be made. Priorities need to be set. And our decisions ultimately have to be incorporated in order to have any benefit, at all.

So, then, what are the standard measures? They are—as former Secretary of Education, William J. Bennett, says—those common characteristics that history itself has proven to be worthwhile. They are not subject to race, color, or creed. There are no laws against them in any country, and they are universally respected by young and old. They are those things which Life itself condones as good, by showering such individuals that adhere to them with good things. And they flourish on **common ground.**

Good people live on common ground. They do not hide, shirk their duties, or interfere in the lives of others who live there. And the startling thing is, that if a poll was taken that could encompass everyone on the planet, we would find that most people live on this common ground. That's because it is part of our basic humanity to gravitate toward these good things. It's human nature.

In bringing up children, it is often tempting to get caught up in the temporary struggles that are merely stepping-stones to maturity, as opposed to promoting the standards that will ultimately strengthen the maturing process. Many times a child is corrected or even excused from offending behavior because of their age or disposition, when they are not only capable, but happier, when given a more general rule to live by.

For instance, if Jimmy pushes his little sister because she stepped in front of him while he was watching TV, it isn't very beneficial to smack him for being rough, or let her push him back so that he "knows how it feels." What he learns from this type of response is that he will be more careful not to get caught next time.

However, if he is admonished that no one likes to be pushed because it breaks one of our most important rules—which is to be kind to each other—and we must look for a better way of communicating disturbances other than being physical, we now have a situation that his heart can respond to. It is not wrong to be irritated at someone for getting in your way. It is wrong to be unkind. He should have asked her to move, or moved himself, in order to solve the problem.

> *It is wrong to be unkind.*

A time out away from others (and the TV) is an appropriate consequence, here, in order to demonstrate that the welfare of others is always more important than television. This doesn't mean he has to remain in this banishment for a half an hour or more. Five to fifteen minutes will do (depending on the age of the child), and when he returns, the incident is forgiven and forgotten, which demonstrates kindness to him in return.

Every once in a while, it becomes necessary for families to take stock of their own personal standards, and to do a little readjusting if they have slipped into some habits that don't quite measure up. Following are some guidelines to help decide whether your rules are really promoting your family values, or not.

MEASURE BY VIRTUE. Patience, kindness, tolerance, and consideration… these are some of the qualities that not only make family life better, they make whole societies better. And contrary to popular opinion, these traits do not show weakness. They produce a strength of character that is admired in every culture.

AVOID PETTINESS. Is an infraction important enough to bring a consequence based on principle? If it isn't, don't complain about it. If you don't want kids yelling in the house today because you have a headache, find a better way to communicate that you would appreciate a little peace and quiet other than yelling, "Stop yelling in the house!"

RESPECT OTHERS and your children will not only respect others, they will respect you. No one likes to be called names, and most employees would be irate if the boss insulted them or their work in front of co-workers. Children feel the same way.

DON'T IGNORE ISSUES. Many parents wait until disagreements turn into brawls before intervening. If you become aware of inappropriate behavior going on, diffuse it before it escalates. Bad behavior isn't going to get any better by getting worse first.

ENCOURAGE GOOD character traits whenever you see them demonstrated in your family. If you do, they will show up more often.

INSIST ON SHARING. It is one of the best disciplines that Life has to offer. Regular practice not only makes others happier, it instills compassion, thoughtfulness, and the ability to be gratified by someone else's pleasure.

BE AN EXAMPLE. Don't ask your children to do anything

you don't require of yourself. Children are mirrors of their parent's values, not models of behavior.

It is important to promote family values in bringing up children. Not only because they make life better, but because things of value last. Simple habits like making a bed a certain way, or washing vegetables before storing them in the refrigerator have a degree of benefit but they tend to disappear with the individual.

As much as women have been liberated in many ways since women's suffrage and the equal rights amendments, history is full of women who ruled nations, fought wars, and became wealthy long before any of those laws were passed in Congress. They did those things because of who they were on the inside. Which not only earned them the admiration of others, but illuminated the paths of others that followed after them. Their inner values never died.

Those same values can not only be developed today, they can still be found producing the same kind of results. So, if you find yourself struggling with what is—or isn't—worth teaching your children in this day and age; decide first if the lasting effect will have any value, or not. Then remember a person doesn't have to be intelligent or wealthy, or even what we tend to call "an ordinary parent" in order to teach their children the greatest values of all time. It's done every day by people all over the world.

Simply by showing them how to live on "*common ground.*"

23

The Meaning of Things

Children are great mimics. They can capture attitudes, body language, and parrot phrases with the skill of impressionists before they hit the age of five. This can be highly entertaining at social gatherings. But like all childhood talents, the lines between when and where, real and unreal, and what's appropriate and what isn't are way beyond the capacity of most children to distinguish. This is made up for by their driving need for approval, which—for the most part—keeps them reeled in close to what their parents would or wouldn't allow. Which pretty much covers things in a social setting.

What goes on at home is another matter.

If it is true that children will mimic attitudes and phrases, it should come as no surprise that they will also successfully display the appropriate behavior patterns that parents require of them. And they will do it without having the slightest idea of why or what they are doing it for. As far as they are concerned, they are doing it for you, and that's reason enough.

There are a lot of things children don't understand but this amazing aptitude for mimicry helps them to get by nicely until they do. Even if they never do, the talent will help them get by adequately in almost any life situation, except maybe running for president. The point is, about thirty percent of the words we use to communicate with children, are words that children do not know the meaning of.

A simple test is to ask a child under ten to define the word "attitude." Most can't. And even though they might hear this word frequently in the phrase, "You better change your attitude!" they have worked out their own acceptable response for it. To them, it means whatever activity they are involved in is to stop immediately. The result of which is usually agreeable to the parent, so nothing further is mentioned. The phrase itself could be just as easily exchanged with, "Straighten up!" and produce the same results. One might argue that it makes no difference as long as the desired effect is achieved. But it does. For like planting seeds, most of those differences won't show up until later on down the road.

They show up in the form of "not being able to get through to the child" as easy as it was when they were younger. In the next stage of development, they aren't quite as driven to please. Not because they feel any less for their parents, but because their world has expanded, and the distraction and excitement it offers are much more interesting than the old home-place. Even if it's a nice one. Which is how it should be, for we ultimately want our children to grow up and stand on their own, and this stage is simply part of the process.

It is also the place where if you have neglected to teach

certain communication skills in the earlier years, it will be twice as hard to do at this point. A child has a stronger sense of self at this later stage; along with a tendency to resent someone else planting seeds in their garden when they are so driven to do it themselves. Not that it can't be done. It just takes a little more time and care not to bruise tender egos.

It has been said that one should never assume anything. But there are certain situations in the parent/child relationship when it is vital to do just that. The difference here is not to assume that your children understand you, but rather to assume that they don't. Which often reveals the need to sharpen up on a few of your own communication skills in order to help them.

Sadly, many failures to communicate are not met with an additional effort to make things clearer. Instead, we fall back on statements like, "What's the matter with you?" or "What were you thinking?" Which, in turn, leaves the child thinking there must be something wrong with what they did. Or worse, yet, with who they are. Few parents realize that the communication breakdown might be on their end, and if they do, feel little need to make things right. They think if their children don't know by now what their parents expect, they better learn.

And most children do. The trouble with this scenario is—though it spreads a seeming peace for the time being—it tends to perpetuate poor communication skills from one generation to another. Something that can cause more problems not only the older one gets but the farther along one gets in life. Many an executive is stopped on his or her way up the corporate ladder simply by a lack of communication skills.

Which doesn't mean parents should panic and start reading

the Wall Street Journal, or "*How To Win Friends and Influence People*" in order to assure that their children will succeed in life (though of course, neither of these fine publications could hurt). It just means that every now and then, one should take an assessment of how things are proceeding in the communication department of your family and then make a few adjustments if need be.

Here are some suggestions to help:

TEST THE WATERS of your communication habits by asking every now and then for your child to tell you what a certain word in your instructions means. For instance, if Johnny's teeth-brushing routine has come up lacking again, after agreeing to do a "thorough job" of it, you better ask him what he thinks the meaning of *thorough* is. In his book, it might simply be using enough toothpaste to pass the breath test. The same can be said of the five-year-old girl who memorized The Lord's Prayer, but changed the phrase "daily bread" to "jelly bread" when she recited it in front of her Sunday school teacher. As far as she was concerned, she had never tasted anything called *daily* before.

NEVER PASS UP A CHANCE TO EXPLAIN THINGS. The way things work, why people do things, the way you do things in your own home—and why—are all things children need to know but rarely ask about. What's more, if you can engage them in a discussion at the same time, you will not only be sharing important knowledge with them, you will be giving them valuable practice in expressing themselves... which is the all-important first step in the communication process.

TEACH YOUR CHILDREN TO LISTEN. With so many things vying for a child's attention these days, it isn't uncommon to find a child who can't keep his mind—much less his ears—focused on anything. And although many children have a capacity to grasp what is being said to them while doing something else at the same time, it is a trait that gets a negative response instead of a positive one in the rest of society. Especially at school. There are three important things that show others you are listening. Here they are:

* Always maintain *eye contact* with who is speaking.

* *Nod* every now and then to show that you understand.

* Give an appropriate answer or response to *acknowledge when the person is finished speaking.*

A person who masters these three listening skills, no matter how old they are, is well on their way to being respected by others. Here are some other things that will help, too:

USE COMMON COURTESIES when speaking with your children and they will use them with you and others. Excuse me, please and thank you, and calling each other by name, cultivates respect. And respect cultivates the desire to listen. A person can have the best communication skills there are but if the person they are talking to isn't listening, they might as well be talking to themselves.

> *Yelling automatically puts the recipient in a deeensive psition.*

AVOID YELLING to make your point. Yelling automatically puts the recipient in a defensive position as opposed to a receptive one... which would you prefer?

NEVER WITHHOLD AFFECTION AS A MEANS OF DISAPPROVAL. If you disapprove of your child's behavior or attitude—tell them. Or give them an appropriate consequence. Withholding touch or friendliness is a form of rejection, not disapproval. Especially for young ones.

DON'T OVER-EXPLAIN. Try to be sensitive to your child's age, attention span, and frame of mind when you want to go into lengthy explanations of things. Like the parent who went into a detailed description of the lifecycle when their child's question of, "Where did I come from?" really meant he was only wondering which city he was born in (as opposed to what his literal origins were). A lack of communication can be as much the fault of a parent as a child.

> *All children are tender-heartted.*

ALWAYS ASSUME THAT YOUR CHILDREN ARE TENDER-HEARTED, no matter what their reactions to you (or any given situations) are. All children are tender hearted.

Though one doesn't have to be skilled in the art of communication in order to survive in life, one can definitely get along better and happier if they are. Teaching the basic habits of communication in the early years while it is natural for children to imitate will not only be easier—it will make communicating easier for them when they are past the formative years. Why? Because everyone responds to good communication skills, no matter what age, race, color, or creed they are. It's human nature.

Children who have learned these things from an early age will continue to practice them *by habit*. Habits that others will —by nature—respond to. What's more, they can be a real safeguard during the later "unlovely years" when our darlings are more involved with themselves than others, which is also human nature.

And human nature is much easier to deal with when you consider the true meaning of things.

The Pursuit Of Excellence

24

A Matter of Taste

It's easy to be picky these days. Not only do we have much to choose from, our modern lifestyles have virtually eliminated the inconvenience of living differently than others. Even within the same family. And while this is a boon to those with separate schedules, it can also be a bane to children who never get practice at putting the needs and preferences of others ahead of their own. Which is extremely important in the long-term scheme of things.

The ability to postpone self-gratification—for any reason—widens horizons. It puts the brain in control over the body. Which is a wonderful knack to acquire, considering the body is purely responsive, while the brain possesses that marvelous power we call deductive reasoning. "If I do this, that will happen. If I don't, then..." and so on. Which can be a handy thing for a child when deciding to carry out a specific action that would probably send parents through the roof if they found out about it.

Much of deductive reasoning is a joint venture in the parent/child relationship during the early years. Yet, most of the foundation for a child's later abilities to reason is based upon those early experiences. That isn't to say the thinking process cannot be changed after the age of five, it simply takes a greater effort to do so. If you are a parent who allows your four-year-old to live off macaroni and cheese without any vegetables on the side because it's easier than putting up with the tantrums, the confrontation you will get from her at fourteen (with socially hazardous things) will be multiplied along with her years. Although most parents will agree that a confrontation with a four-year-old is much easier to deal with than one with a teenager, it's surprising how many parents will opt to avoid it.

Just for the short-term benefits.

Which brings us back to the pros and cons of being picky, again. The truth is, everybody is picky in some way or another. It's human nature. But the thing that sets the nature of humans above that of animals is an amazing ability to be able to choose what you will be picky about. One can even change their tastes if they feel so inclined, something that opens up a whole new world when it comes to achieving goals.

The ability to use deductive reasoning on future events is an ability only humans are capable of. The other life forms we share our planet with must make do with their "response-abilities." Yet, there are no "deductive reasoning police" roaming about to enforce whether we are using too much or too little of it. We can live like the animals if we so choose. Or, we can fly to the moon. The choice is entirely up to the individual. It is also true that within every individual—no matter how they choose to live or behave—lies the latent ability to do great things. Yet, most never do.

Why is that?

Because even though we are all living every day with the consequences of our choices, most of us do not realize that we can change any of it. Much less how to go about it. Oddly enough, it is not a matter of intelligence but one of perspective. It's one of those cases where it's difficult to see the forest because of all the trees. The power to change life comes from the knowledge that different choices will bring different results. The courage to do so comes from experience. Let's say practice. And anything practiced from an early age becomes part of our...

Nature.

Behind the laws of nature (which we seem to hem ourselves in with) lie the forces of nature, which we know very little about. Other than the fact that they are powerful and more than a little intimidating. They have even been referred to as "acts of God" because of their propensity to override everything in their path when headed in a certain direction. A force is a source of power, whereas a law is merely a declaration that a power exists.

For instance, the phrase "What goes up must come down," is one of the most common references to a law of nature. Which is mostly true. Yet, by applying the theories of aeronautics, man has proven that it is not only possible to override this law but has rendered it common practice by making air travel a part of our modern-day lives.

The forces of nature hold many such "overrides" to otherwise natural hindrances and they are freely available to anyone who has the desire and determination to use them. The people that do, seem to accomplish so much more than others that society has a tendency to call them gifted. The real secret is that they have simply spent a lot of time practicing what they have become so good at. To do this, they have chosen not to do something else, in order to achieve their goals.

Here are seven natural overrides that—when practiced—have the power to produce "gifted" children:

DETERMINATION ALWAYS OVERRIDES TALENT. It is amazing how many famous historical figures did not have their origins in the halls of the rich and famous. In fact, many of them had more obstacles to overcome than the average person. But the common thread that runs through the lives of all of them is an uncanny determination to do whatever they set out to. There is an old saying that tells us, "The world steps aside for any man who knows where he is going," which is still true today. So, how do we create determination? Encourage your children to try and keep on trying. And if one thing doesn't work, try it again a different way.

LOOK FOR THE GOOD. A single day can only contain so much, so we have to pick and choose what we will fill it with. Good things to do, to talk about, to think on, not only make a person happier, they make other people happy when they are around them. A smile always overrides a frown. A friend is better company than a bully. And good food makes you feel good even after the mealtime is over.

ESTABLISH THE IMPORTANCE OF BEST. The better choice is always the best choice. Encourage your children to make good choices by making it worth their while when they do. If Johnny isn't wild about tomatoes, that doesn't mean he should never have to eat a fresh salad again. The practice (continual repetition) of eating a portion of it each time it is served will be much easier to enforce if you balance it out with fifteen minutes of extended play time, or dessert, or something else he enjoys. This lesson has more benefit to it than nutrition. Subconsciously, it teaches a child that he is capable of trading something unpleasant now, for something that is much more pleasant later. It stretches the ability to endure... which is a forerunner of that all-important trait of determination.

INSTILL THE VALUE OF OTHERS. Sharing, helping, and being careful of the feelings of others has a boomerang effect: it makes the giver feel good, too. Long-term practice of such habits will promote compassion and develop leadership skills.

PLACE AN IMPORTANCE ON KNOWLEDGE. Whoever said, "Knowledge is power" was not far wrong. The more one knows, the more they understand, and with understanding comes the ability to bring the pieces of life's puzzle into a recognizable order. And no matter where it is established, order always brings two cousins along... peace and contentment.

ENCOURAGE PRACTICE: IT MAKES PERFECT. And it takes time. Since whatever one spends the most time at becomes most valuable to them, parents have an opportunity here to choose the best for their children in the early years. Worthwhile activities in the early years provide safeguards for the later ones. That's because any love developed for something at an early age, lasts.

AIM HIGH. Never tell a child they are not smart enough, beautiful enough, or rich enough to do anything. Every child comes equipped with more than enough ability to do great things. The only thing that can hinder them is a lack of belief in themselves: a condition brought on mostly by what others tell them they cannot do.

Why should children eat well? Because they will be stronger, brighter, and happier if they do. Why should they be kind to others? Because they will be stronger, brighter, and happier if they do. Why should they learn anything extra if they don't have to? Because they will be stronger, brighter and happier if they do.

Learning to choose well can make a big difference in life, and knowing that tastes and feelings will change according to your choices (if you practice enough) can make anything possible in your future. What's more, any parent who chooses to reveal this wonderful secret to their children will not only be a participant in wonderful and amazing things, they will also open doors for the "gifted" to pass through.

> *It is the nature of children to take whatever is given to them.*

The thing about a gift is, it is given by someone else. And since parents tend to give more gifts than anyone else in a child's life, it becomes vitally important to be picky about just what those gifts will be. Someone who consistently gives good gifts is admired in our societies and said to have developed "good taste." Although it is still up to the individual to decide whether or not to use their gifts, it is the nature of children to take whatever is given to them. And as with all gifts, the choice of what that gift will be is entirely up to the giver. We all know there are good gifts and bad ones.

It's simply a matter of taste.

25

Doing What's Best

It isn't always easy to know what's best for your children. Especially in situations that neither of you have experienced before. And contrary to popular opinion, a parent's instinct is often in conflict with a child's natural tendencies. What's more, it is sometimes difficult to get a handle on instinct when some end up convinced they don't possess any of it, at all. Children, on the other hand, are never at a lack for natural tendencies.

The thing about children is, they force you to deal with certain issues whether you're ready, or not. Usually, it's not. Most of us, given the choice to avoid certain issues, would definitely opt for a way of getting around them. That's because it seems no amount of planning or preparation (or money, or lack of it) can prepare you for a baby that suddenly vomits in a crowded elevator, or a teenager who decides to swim naked in a friend's pool and gets caught. Though we all end up living through these kinds of experiences, the majority of us are never prepared for the actual moments of their occurrence.

The phrase "It is amazing what children can survive,"

> *Raising children is an emotional business.*

should also be applied to parents. No one seems to get through the years it takes to raise a child without a significant list of the incidents that have "given them gray hairs" along the way. That's because raising children is an emotional business, whether you happen to be overly emotional, or not.

Yet, outside of perfunctory greetings and bedtime routines, the emotional side of parenting is often the most ignored and least talked about aspect of the entire parent/child process. No one likes being emotional. Except maybe teenagers, who seem to thrive on strong feelings, whether they might be joy, anger, fear, or despair. The stronger the better. Which is a study in itself.

The truth is, all humans are emotional. Some of them just keep it to themselves more than others. And some of them are so skilled at not showing any response, they convince those around them they are not as sensitive as most people. Which is a deception. A very good, self-inflicted one, but a deception, none-the-less. All humans are born with a working set of emotions in the same way they are born with completely functioning hearts, livers, and lungs. You can't see any of these organs at work from the outside, either, but we know they are working, just the same. It's that way with emotions.

In the same way it helps to understand the physical stages of a child's growth to better meet their needs, it also helps to have a better understanding of the intricate nature of their emotions. For the very same reason. That's because emotionally depraved children turn into dysfunctional adults, later on in life. Which isn't good for anybody.

The famous study that involved war orphans after the last world war showed that infants who merely had their physical needs met, eventually weakened and died. It wasn't enough to be merely fed and clothed, they also had to be held and comforted, and to make some sort of emotional contact with at least one other human being in order to have the necessary impetuous to survive. In the same way, children who are abused by others have a tendency to shut themselves off from outside stimulus and, if the situation is prolonged, become harder and harder for anyone to reach, mentally as well as physically.

So, it would seem that even in infant stages, children possess a sort of will over their own response mechanisms that allows them to adapt to individual situations. On the negative side, these are mostly defense mechanisms that operate in much the same way the physical body does when met with intense physical pain or trauma: it simply shuts down. On the positive side, however, this same "will" can be so nurtured and encouraged as to produce some of the finest human beings of our times.

What makes some people great, and others simply content to survive?

The answer lies somewhere in this mysterious part of humanity we refer to as the individual will, which has its greatest influence from the emotions. A look at our great heroes of history shows that they spring from all walks of life. It seems to make little difference if they were born rich or poor, or even what country they come from. The truth is, most of those unique individuals ultimately complete their destinies after having overcome incredible personal odds. In military archives, it has been proven over and over again that men lay down their lives for their comrades, not for their ideals... giving us another fleeting glimpse of the importance of emotions in human relationships.

Yet, how many times have we heard phrases like, "I put food on the table and pay the bills, for heaven sake—that alone should be enough to prove that I love my children." No, it isn't. There is also a popular saying that says, "Actions speak louder than words." But when it comes to emotions, this isn't true, either. Words are the most potent vehicles for emotions known to humanity. If abused children can, and do, continue to love and be loyal to abusive parents simply because the guilt-ridden offender lavishes on declarations of love and sorrow afterward, how much more can parents who are normal achieve with the same emphasis of expression? Oddly enough, many of these normal parents don't feel that such encounters are even necessary. But they are.

> *Words are the most potent vehicles for emotions known to humanity.*

There are certain drives in the emotional psyche of a human being that are universal. They are to feel accepted, to be loved, and to have someone or something to live for. The results of having these basic emotional needs met, are that the individual will in turn be accepting of others, know how to love someone else, and develop the amazing ability to set themselves aside for higher ideals. They will lean more toward being contributing citizens of our society instead of just consumers. So, considering the importance of these things to not only our future generations but the individual quality of life itself, how does a parent go about promoting them?

Here are some suggestions that can help:

A Quiet place is a rarity in today's noisy society, especially in a child's world. We seem to think that rowdy and constantly active is the nature of children and even find ourselves contributing to ways of keeping them so occupied. Yet, it is essential for children to have moments of quiet to contemplate themselves, the world around them, and simply to observe the life process in order to develop their reasoning powers for later life. What was Columbus doing when he made his famous observation that the sails of ships seemed to sink below the horizon line instead of fall off of it? Certainly not playing a game of stickball.

A point of acceptance is the bottom line for any child. To be assured that they are loved unconditionally no matter what they look like or how they behave is the fundamental basis of security for children. Because of this, discipline and communication should never intrude here. Contrary to popular opinion, being a permanently accepted member of the family has nothing to do with unacceptable behavior on a daily basis: they are two different things altogether.

A space to grow in. As parents, we seldom like to acknowledge the fact that our children are growing up. And many of the misunderstandings of the teen years stem from a parent refusing to accept the fact that their child is closer to adulthood than childhood. What's more, we also have a propensity to not let them forget their younger shortcomings which—many times—they have long since grown out of. A parent who can provide "a little space for stretching" instead of waiting until their child grows uncomfortable, will be ahead of the game. Have a teenager who is getting so close to driving age you are dreading the day he asks to give it a try? Then "buck up" and offer him the experience before he has to ask. Guess who will end up the hero?

A physical contact. All people need physical contact. It's human nature. Hug, touch, sit next to, and hold your kids... forever.

A mental avenue. The human mind responds to stimulation in the same way that the body responds to exercise. A child who is encouraged from early on to "think about things" will not only resort to this in adulthood, they'll get smarter. That's because most of what we call smart is simply a storehouse of experience.

An emotional attachment. Everybody needs at least one of these in their life. So, give your kids a jump-start and make things easier for them by giving as many opportunities as you can for the experience. Think pets (or siblings, or in-laws, or best friends overnight) are too much work? Get a grip and give in. The investment pays great dividends in the long run.

Something to dream about is what ignites the brain, the heart, and the energy like nothing else in life can. Many high achievers have been dreaming about certain goals from an amazingly early age. Never be too quick to "pour cold water" on elaborate declarations of desires to be the next astronaut, or even the next president. All the astronauts and presidents there ever were started off by being somebody's kid who lived next door.

So, if you ever find yourself feeling on the short end of always knowing what's best for your children, you can take comfort in the fact that nobody else does, either. It is not a prerequisite of parenthood to understand the whole meaning and miracle of life; only to be a responsible caregiver for your own miraculous part in it, which is the child you personally ushered into the world.

In the same way that the farmer who plants his crop does not worry that his corn might come up oats or wheat this time—or maybe nothing at all—the process of children changing into adults takes place whether they have good parents or bad ones. And just as rich soil, sunlight, and water are known to produce the best crops once the seed is in the ground; providing "fertile ground" for meeting the emotional as well as the physical needs of your children will produce the same kind of quality in your kids. The rest is up to nature.

That's really all there is to doing what's best.

26

Doing Things On Purpose

Doing things "on purpose" is serious stuff. Children who break things or hurt someone seem to know that if they didn't do it on purpose—if it was accidental—the consequences for such actions will be much lighter. And they usually are. Webster's dictionary defines the word purpose as "taking direct aim or intention," and anything begun in this manner is almost always carried through. It's human nature.

To have purpose sparks determination in ways nothing else can because it comes directly from the individual and not outside influences. Yet, it is so natural to human growth and development that parents often overlook opportunities to utilize it in other areas. We seem to recognize it "in stages" as opposed to individual qualities. For instance, a child who shows an amazing amount of determination as a toddler will also possess amazing amounts as a teen. In fact, he will have the same levels available to him throughout his entire life, although what he chooses to do with it is another subject.

Purpose brings with it an incredible amount of staying power. It is an attention holder. There are many things in the course of a day that can catch your attention but few that manage to hold onto it for very long. To be involved in something of purpose is one of the few instances in life where the human mind and body can actually set time aside. Eating and sleeping have been known to take a backseat when the mind is intent on accomplishing something. What's more, there are few gratifications in life that are as potent as the accomplishment of something one has purposed to do.

> *Purpose brings with it an incredible amount of staying power.*

This being the case, it is rather startling how many of us meander through weeks, months, and even years, without dipping into this wonderful well. And children are no different. When you detect irritabilities on the rise and enthusiasms beginning to wane, you've got fertile ground for doing things on purpose. A parent who recognizes this and can provide something worthwhile during these situations, is doing much more than maintaining a momentary satisfaction: he is teaching his children how to manufacture their own.

Yet, how does one know—especially when it comes to children's activities—which ones are truly worthwhile, or not? The secret lies in what things are worthwhile for your particular child. That's because what is engrossing for one could very well be boring for another. And sometimes the most mundane for most people can end up being the catalyst for genius in someone else. Such as Bowditch's uncommon fascination for numbers at a remarkably early age, Disney's propensity for dreaming and "doodling" as a young boy, and Mozart's perfect ear for the musical scale at the age of four.

Keeping a watchful eye on your child's responses to the world going on around them can give you a key to unlocking those special interests, within, that they might not even be aware of themselves. Here are some things to look for:

SIGNS OF INTENSITY. There's a difference between a child who is completely caught up in an activity and one who is merely enjoying the participation. Are they blocking out things that are going on at the same time and giving it their full attention? Do they have the patience to keep at it longer than most? Do they want to do it over and over? That's intensity.

A SPECIAL KNACK. Are you rather surprised at how fast your child caught onto something or offered a timely suggestion that no one else thought of? Do certain activities or thought processes seem to come easy to them when most must work a bit harder to achieve the same level of accomplishment? These things are often an indication that a higher level in the same area would offer a more satisfying challenge than doing something different altogether.

OFFER A VARIETY. Children are often as surprised as we are when they discover a new talent or enjoyable pastime. Many times they are the very last ones to know what they really want or would like to do. Giving them opportunity to try different things not only gives them a wider selection to choose from, it also helps to eliminate those things that they have no interest in, at all.

PROVIDE MATERIALS. There are many children who would progress amazingly far in certain areas if only they had the appropriate stimulating materials to work with. Do you have a child that's uncommonly interested in science? Don't just praise them for a job well done at school: provide them with things at home that they can continue to explore with. Microscopes, telescopes, tiny motors and switches hold much more fascination for children with inquiring minds than toys that look like, but don't really do the real thing that they are supposed to.

ENCOURAGE COMMUNICATION. Ask them to explain their projects and ideas to you. Sometimes, it is in trying to explain things to others that make them clearer in our own minds. It's the same with children. The more they talk about things, the more enthusiastic they become, then enthusiasm fuels the fires of purpose.

DON'T BELITTLE SMALL THINGS. Did your children just spend the entire afternoon digging a hole for who knows why? Then before you make comments about "what for" or what a mess they made, take note of the fact at how well they worked together, or the size of what they accomplished. Think of things one could do with such a hole. You might even go so far as to allow them to dig all the holes they want, as long as they fill each one back in, again, when they are through.

CHOOSE PURPOSE FIRST. If you put a priority on things your child finds purpose in over pastimes that are more conveniently at hand, neither of you will be sorry. The length of time they will stay at these things will stretch to longer and longer intervals, cutting down on the length of time you have to spend coming up with other things for them to do when they are bored.

Children who have put their whole effort into accomplishing something—and do it—are not afraid to tackle things in other situations, either. A child who is allowed to stimulate and develop their mental processes will carry their advancements into the classroom setting, as well. And children that spend more time "on purpose" have an easier time figuring out where to go when they become adults.

Positively speaking, there's a lot to be said for doing things on purpose.

27

About Time

As any successful businessman will tell you, "Time is money." And if we would put the same value on the time we invest in our children, the results would be equally profitable. Maybe even more. One of the characteristics of wealthy people is that they are very careful with their money. They rarely squander it even though they can afford to. Instead they are more profit-driven, always opting for the deal that will be the most advantageous for them in the long run. The same can be said of successful parenting. Though one does not have to be wealthy to be a successful parent, many of the same principals apply.

Such as a budget.

One also does not have to be wealthy to know that if you do not designate a specific place for your money to go every month, it will leave you wondering where it went when that month is over. It is the same with raising children. "Where did the time go?" is the most frequently asked question of parents whose children have grown up and moved out on their own.

The Nature Of Children

One of the most common characteristics of successful parents is that, somewhere along the line, they have been very specific about where their children spend their time. They are usually the ones that have said, "You may watch television after you have practiced your piano lesson," or "read a book for an hour," or "done your homework." They are the ones who make sure there is enough time left in the evening for cultivating good habits like bathing, laying out clothes for tomorrow, and cleaning up any games or projects that have been participated in. But how does one go about doing that in this fast-paced day and age?

By budgeting your children's time.

You begin the same as you would with a money budget: by making a list of your assets and liabilities. What are Jenny's assets? Let's say, she is intelligent, has a long attention span, and is very social. Her liabilities are a volatile temper when she crosses her frustration limit and an out-and-out stubbornness when she can't have her way. She also talks too much in school. For the sake of a good example, let's make this a family budget and give Jenny a brother. Johnny is also intelligent, very athletic, and good at figuring out mechanical things. On the other hand, he can't seem to sit still for more than twenty minutes at a stretch, argues about everything, and is a merciless tease.

Following along with our money guidelines, we must now decide what to do with our assets, and determine just how much time we are going to pay toward liabilities each month. It is also good to keep an eye out for any opportunities to consolidate whenever we get the chance. Since both children are intelligent, we are going to consolidate the investment toward that intelligence into one fund. Such as music lessons.

Not that one needs to be intelligent to take music lessons. But music bears a striking resemblance to math and has the capacity to fulfill an intelligent child's drive to figure things out. The same is true of playing chess, as opposed to a board game where the entire outcome is left mostly up to chance. In dealing with intelligent children, a parent must always opt for the activity that most stretches the brain. If Johnny is good at sports, he should be allowed to participate in a community league such as soccer or baseball.

Jenny should belong to Girl Scouts, or some similar club-type activity that offers interaction with others. Because of her long attention span, she should always have a long term project going; such as sewing or journal-keeping. Johnny should get involved with electronics or building models. In terms of liabilities, each child should be put on a program that allows sufficient opportunity to work toward changing those unwanted behaviors.

Any time that is left over in the family schedule after all of the above responsibilities have been met, goes into the same category as "mad money" or "miscellaneous." This should be the only fund from which we draw enough accrued time for such things as television, video games, or simply playing. If you find yourself constantly looking for things to occupy your children, chances are, they do not have enough challenging stimulation in their lifestyle. Instead of looking for more—or bigger and better—things, try to determine their individual needs more specifically. Then you can be more on-target when you are budgeting their time. Remember, not every child will respond the same way to the same things.

Following is a list of suggestions that can help you turn more of your children's time into worthwhile time.

RESPECT INDIVIDUAL DIFFERENCES. If Johnny loves his piano lessons but you have to send the "piano Gestapo" out for Jenny whenever practice time rolls around, maybe she will have a stronger interest in something else. It isn't a matter of right or wrong. It simply takes trying many different things, sometimes, in order to find out what the favorites are.

NEVER MAKE ACHIEVEMENT THE RULE. If Johnny isn't a track star, don't berate him for coming in fifth in the hundred yard dash: he might be better at tennis or baseball. In the same way, never criticize one of your little darlings for freezing up during a music recital. The love and mastery of an instrument doesn't always have to include a public career... most of them don't.

LET THEM STAND ALONE. Many parents try to fulfill their own dreams and desires through their children. Which is perfectly natural, especially when so many character traits are passed along from one generation to the next. But every once in a while, parents can be almost certain that an alien was somehow deposited in their midst instead of a natural heir. If dad has always been an avid hunter but his teenaged daughter turns out to be a conservationist, don't put her down for being one. Similarly, if she doesn't want to enter a beauty pageant even though she's cuter than Shirley Temple and her mother once won Miss Idaho, don't make her.

DON'T CRITICIZE. Very few things in life come so natural that one doesn't have to go through a learning process to get good at it. Better not to say anything at all than tell Johnny his rendition of "The Mexican Hat Dance" sounded like Reggae. If you can't say something nice...

DON'T TALK MONEY. Your child should never feel obligated for the money you spend for lessons, or a scout uniform, or anything else you pay for. Other than choosing between one activity or another (if you can't afford both), a child should never be on the executive board of household finances. So, unless you expect your eight-year-old to take up a part-time job in order to pay for his own education, don't make him feel like he should.

BE SUPPORTIVE. Show up at those games and recitals, and be the proud parent your child needs you to be. Help with school activities once in a while if volunteers are needed, and don't give in to the temptation to let someone else's parent do it because they have more time than you. Nobody has more time.

> *Time pays dividends in the same way that money does.*

DISCOURAGE SELFISHNESS. Even though it is important to develop our individual talents and interests, it is never more important than being a good friend and family member. Do you know someone who could take after school lessons if they had transportation? Then offer to lend a hand. Being an example is the best way of teaching your children to care for others as well as themselves... and that makes them better people.

Time pays dividends in the same way that money does. And as with money, people who invest more in something usually get more out of it in the long run. Children have the same amount of time in their day as adults do but they rarely have much choice in where they spend it. That is their parents' decision. A gifted child is usually put into that category because of parents who have already given them not only a gift of recognition of their unique abilities, but the time to pursue it.

The truth is, every child is gifted in some way or another, but they will make do with whatever is set before them. If they live in a junkyard, they will learn to love junk; if they live in a garden, they will love the flowers. If you haven't really ever thought about where your children could be spending their time as opposed to where they actually do...

Then maybe it's about time.

28

The Search for Together

Contrary to popular opinion, together is not a place. It is now possible, more than any other time in history, to be in the same room with someone and not really be with them. An abundance of modern inventions like the television, computers and cell phones are mostly responsible. Then again, it can be argued that it is people who do things and not the things themselves. Which is true. Nevertheless, we have a problem in our day that was of little concern to those of previous eras: we can be here and "gone" at the same time.

While these inventions have turned out to be marvelous babysitters (not to mention spectacular family entertainment), they have also been the very instruments that have robbed parents of a great part of the force of their natural influence. Not only can we bring the world inside our homes for our children to play in, they are often more influenced by where they are playing than with us.

It's a trade-off we originally went into with our eyes wide open when mothers first started taking full time jobs outside the home. Someone has to mind the children while she is catching up on her cooking or cleaning she missed out on during the workday. And most of us send up praise to the heavens for films and games that are so captivating to children they get the job done with flying colors. The trouble is, we don't stop with our cooking and cleaning time.

While the entertainment industry is wonderful at its job with children, it is also equally wonderful at doing the same thing with tired adults. We have traded much of the nurturing aspects of parenting for something called "bonding time." Which is supposed to be taking place while we are merely engaged in being entertained together. A bona fide substitute: until the entertainment industry comes up with clashing values. Something it frequently does. Like presenting a beautiful picture of life "in the fast lane" for teens, or flashing close-up shots of king-size aliens that bear a striking resemblance to the insect world mutated with some form of human, during the dinner hour. A surprising number of family dinner hours are frequently spent in front of the television.

As parents, we have combated most of these onslaughts with declarations of "they are not real." Which goes over about as well as a lead balloon, considering the children saw it with their own eyes only moments ago. What's more, the very same vision can be conjured up in the most horrifying of moments, unannounced. Like when Mom or Dad turn the lights out at bedtime.

When even Disney's beloved characters, Pooh and Eyore, can have scary adventures by falling through a mysterious hole under the bed, many bedrooms that should represent a haven of warmth and security have transformed themselves into nightmare proportions. One of the results of this phenomenon is that the amount of time parents spend in dealing with such childhood phobias far exceed the time that it used to take before such things existed.

Frustrations ensue for both parent and child.

Often it seems like most of our time interacting with our children consists of settling problems. Which is not how it was meant to be. A work-worn mom who knows better for reasons she is too tired to concentrate on, much less articulate, is no match for the well-dressed savvy parent of the latest sitcom who seems to have no trouble letting her children live their own lives and work out their own problems. Except in real life, children rarely have the best ideas on how to work out their own problems.

It is also a fallacy that running errands, visiting friends, or going to children's sports events is spending quality time together. The word quality has been inserted here for the mere fact that even wild animals will accept the presence of human beings when not threatened. Thus, it is possible to have a seemingly tranquil period together, when—in all honesty—you are not really together. It is similar to the time an eminent author of children's literature decided to spend a hot southern summer writing on the shady front porch of her home.

Early on in the season she noticed a black snake coiled up on a corner rafter. Deciding that she was outdoors and the snake was indifferent to her, they could both share the porch. Which they did throughout the summer. Soon the snake became such a common sight on the porch in various locations: on the handrail, coiled around a post, in a far-off corner of the floor... that she became as indifferent to the snake as it was to her. One morning, however, when she was reaching for something else, she moved too quickly for the snake's liking... and it bit her. The serpent slithered away into the grass never to return. At which point she decided it was highly unnatural for snakes and people to be friends. An understanding was not enough between them, especially when it was discovered that the rules for that understanding were different for both.

True togetherness is interaction. And positive togetherness that has real bonding quality to it is interaction that has a positive outcome. Bonding means when two separate entities meld together. Two people sitting in the same room do not naturally go through a bonding process. If that were true, then everyone who ever experienced the waiting room in a doctor's office would be expert in the art of human interaction. Does that mean we should turn off the TV entirely and jump into a quest for the purer things in life? Not at all. Television is a lot like dessert: while it adds a great deal of pleasure to the menu, too much of it tends to make people sick. The important thing is not to neglect human nature at the same time.

> *True togetherness is interaction.*

There is no personal commitment in sitting in the same room with someone. But there is in sitting close enough to touch or hold them. Physical contact of any kind with any human being constitutes interaction of the most intimate variety. There will be a positive or negative outcome, one way or the other. You are two people sharing a single space of experience and you are together in that space. Together is sharing. Whether it is space, time, conversation—or even trauma—togetherness is experiencing something at the same time someone else does.

Togetherness is not just exchanging the things you do as a family for something else. It is making sure the things you do exchange offer the kind of human interaction with the right impact. An impact that is often overlooked in today's culture. Following is a list of interactions that spark togetherness, no matter when or where they are done. If you are lacking them, make it a point to implement them in your family, one way or the other, so that you can turn the time you already spend with your children into real bonding time.

> **SHARE THE SAME FOOD.** With all of our convenience foods today, it isn't hard to let personal preferences rule. Yet it is sharing space to eat something that someone else has prepared. What's more, it gives practice in tolerance to be polite enough to eat something someone else has made. Sitting down together and eating it at the same time makes this interaction doubly potent.
>
> **SHARE THE SAME SPACE.** If you can't sit close, touch or hold your child during a viewing activity, at the very least, acknowledge them with a touch or smile at the beginning and end to let them know you are with them in this activity. You will find that through a child's eyes, this is much more important than the activity itself, no matter what they say the first time.
>
> **SHARE THE SAME THOUGHT.** What are they really

saying when they are telling you about their day? Are they avoiding real conversation with the phrase, "Nothing," at your inquiries? Then prompt them with other questions like, "Did you finish your work on time?" "Did you play with anyone in particular at recess?" and other such things in order to engage them in sharing. And remember, if you aren't really listening, they won't bother.

SHARE COURTESIES. Whether you are dealing with toddlers or teens, everyone likes to be acknowledged and listened to. Look your children in the eyes when they are talking, greet them when they are coming or going from a room, and always say, "Goodnight" or "Good morning" every day. If these are the people you care about most in the world, give them the respect of being at least as courteous as you would be to a co-worker.

SHARE YOUR TIME. Time is important to everybody, even children. If you take time out to play with your children, and they, in turn, take their playtime to do things with you, that's interaction of the highest kind. This is where true bonding occurs, and these moments do not go unnoticed by even the youngest of children.

SHARE YOUR KNOWLEDGE. Never pass up the opportunity to tell your children what you know, whether it agrees with the more popular modern-day philosophies, or not. It is the nature of children to listen first and foremost to their parents, and even if they don't acknowledge you at the moment, or meet your offerings with the sigh of, "Oh, Dad!" they will remember it forever. And forever is long enough.

SHARE YOUR LOVE. Never give in to the temptation to assume that your children should know that you love them. Even though you feed, clothe and shelter them from the outside world, these things can be done in such a way that a child feels not love but obligation because of them. No child is obligated to his parents for his daily needs, and you weren't either. Have a hard time saying, "I love you," or expressing how wonderful they are? Then practice. Expressing love for your children is the best thing you can do for them... and you.

Togetherness is not a place. It is a series of interactions between people that brings about bonding in one way or another. Adults need this in order to feel happiness and fulfillment, but children need it in order to grow up into happy, healthy adults that are a credit to the human race instead of a liability. Which is what we would all like to see more of. And if togetherness is something you do, then it stands to reason that the doing of it is merely a decision. Want more of a sense of togetherness in your home? Then decide today to do more of the things that togetherness is.

The effects will be obvious.

Part Four:

Secrets

For Home

29. Three Secrets
30. Just Pretend
31. Back to School Blues
32. Bored with it All
33. Undercover Summers
34. Going to Extremes

Forever

35. Touching Bases
36. Bad Influences
37. Changing Times
38. Owning Your Own Home-life
39. Believe it or Not

For Home

29

Three Secrets

It is no secret that some methods work better than others. The trouble is, when it comes to raising children, there are so many to choose from we sometimes have difficulty recognizing the ones that are best. It is also true that certain things that work well for one person will not always have the same effect on someone else. Personalities differ. Times change. But as stated before in this book…

Human nature never changes.

No matter how old you are, no matter how wise you are, no matter what you like or dislike; there are a few basic things that will always get to you. Along with anyone else that's human. So, why don't we know these things? Why aren't they the first things we learn in life and the last things we forget? Go figure.

It's a mystery. A new age. And these little secrets to life continue to whirl around in the cosmos with the same accuracy and precision as the planets making their perpetual orbits in the sky. And like the planets, you can learn a lot about them by simple observation and contemplation. Only there is precious little time for the observation and contemplation of anything in this day and age beyond what you're having for dinner tonight, and which choice will cost less and go farther in the long run. Especially if you have kids. Which is why the passing along of secrets has become integral to the success and survival of every age and generation since Adam.

You do not have to believe in Adam to know who he is, which just goes to show how far some tidbits of knowledge have been passed down. Without even the aid of a social security number, which most of us wouldn't be caught dead without these days. Especially dead. That's because identity is very important to us humans. Unlike the animals that glory in what they are, we humans are more glorified in who we are. We spend most of our lives just trying to establish that fact. Which leads us to the first of our three secrets:

Acknowledgment.

If it is so vitally important for humans to seek identity, then to acknowledge that identity meets an immediate human need. Every time. You can acknowledge anyone by a look, a touch, or their name spoken out loud. And in this list, the strongest comes last. Let's look a little closer at each of these.

EYE CONTACT. A look means you have given someone your attention, which is an immediate form of acknowledgment. It does not mean you approve. But you know they are there and you are aware of what they are doing. There is always a positive gratification in this, which is why some children (and some adults) will "act out" just to receive it.

TOUCH is the immediate transfer of emotion from one

person to another. It is an intensely personal thing, and therefore no doubt about who it's aimed at, whether negative or positive. It makes a bond which is a stronger form of acknowledgment than a look, which merely makes a connection. You do not give much of yourself away in a look but by touching someone you are conveying an instant message as an enemy or friend. There is seldom any doubt which is which.

To **SPEAK SOMEONE'S NAME** is the highest form of acknowledgment there is. For good, or for bad. It singles them out from the crowd and proves that they are somebody. A name is the first (and last) thing we humans have that is ours and ours alone. What we do in our search for who we are will always be kept within the confines of our very own name. Because of this, it is extremely potent. It is the actual essence of who we are.

So, to acknowledge someone by using their name in a phrase or sentence when speaking to them makes what you are saying more important. Simply because you are giving them positive reinforcement each time you repeat it. The same is true if you are looking directly at, or touching the person you are speaking to. Do you want someone's full attention? Then look them in the eye, touch them in some way, or say their name along with whatever you're talking about.

That's acknowledgment.

The second secret is **recognition**. Personal recognition goes beyond acknowledgment for the simple reason that it always elevates the recipient and never puts them down. To catch a blunt object in mid-swing along with the remark, "Put that thing down, Junior, before you hurt somebody!" will probably not be remembered past tomorrow, much less as one of our treasured childhood moments. On the other hand; to stand Junior on a chair before the rest of the kids, give him a "napkin hat" for a crown, a ladle for a scepter and say, "I present to everybody King Junior, who ate all of his alphabet soup, today!" will go down in family history.

To be formally recognized (no matter how informally you do it) means you not only are somebody, you have actually accomplished something. It strengthens your name. Which is where you keep everything that's you. In the same way, the "welcome courtesies" signify that a person is important enough to be formally recognized when they are coming or going or introduced to a new crowd. Hello and good-bye, good morning and good night, and even "See ya, sweetie!" all fit into this category.

To add these little secrets of recognition to your communication skills makes you more important. Why? Because that's human nature. And the next time you think a handshake or personal greeting doesn't mean much, just look at the politicians. The ones who get out and "greet" the most people get the most votes.

The third secret is **listening**. A good listener never lacks friends. But how can you tell a good listener from a bad one? A good listener always responds to what they are hearing. Here are the most important listening responses:

* Look the speaker in the eye while they are talking.

* Encourage them to continue with occasional verbal agreements such as "Yes... is that right?... Really... Hmmm... etc."

* Nod your head at intervals.

* Every once in a while, repeat something they said back to them. For example, "The dog ate your homework?... Chewed it to little bits, huh... spit it out on the floor?"

> *Being a good listener to others will make others respect you more.*

Being a good listener to others will make others respect you more. People will seek you out in order to have someone to talk to. Before you know it, they will start asking you questions and coming to you for advice. The role of a "counselor" (one who listens and confides) is a very coveted position in the society of human relationships, even though anyone can become one by practicing these few social skills. It's just that most people don't. The truth is, you can give your children a head start in life by teaching them, from an early age, to practice social skills. And remember: what children learn early, they learn well. Here are a few ways to practice social skills in your home:

BE A GOOD EXAMPLE. If you practice these things with your children, they will practice them with you.

DO IT OVER. If the first thing out of Jimmy's mouth in the morning is, "I'm hungry!"—have him come in again and try, "Good morning, Mom. May I have some breakfast, please?" If he's not ready to do that, he's probably not ready for breakfast. So, encourage him to keep trying.

DON'T ALLOW RUDENESS to be acceptable in your home. If Sally calls her brother a "pickle-puss" and sticks out her tongue, don't just say, "No name calling!" Have her apologize and say something nice about him.

LET THEM PRACTICE. When company comes over, introduce your children the same way you would another adult. Encourage them to shake hands, look the visitor in the eye and say, "Hello," or "Nice to meet you." Even if you only have toddlers. No age limits, here... everybody's human.

PRAISE THEM for practicing these things. Verbal acknowledgment, recognition, and attention from you, is worth more to them than anything... so use it to their advantage.

A person does not have to be feeling good, kind, wise, or even "in the mood" to practice good social skills. We just need to make them a habit. In the same way a good driver does not need to constantly be thinking of the rules of the road wherever he goes, a good communicator does not have to always be thinking about manners. Which is really what we're getting down to here. We are living in a time when manners are pretty much optional for daily living. But the fact remains that good manners win out over bad manners—or, even no manners—every time.

Giving your children a skill that will give them an edge every time they use it, will not only build self confidence in them, but will build other's confidence in them, as well. That's the biggest secret to success there is.

30

Just Pretend

The world can get pretty scary sometimes if you're four feet tall or under. In spite of discriminating parents who exercise control over viewing and listening in the house, even momentary flashes of the sort of visual images available these days can linger in the memory for weeks. Coupled with the shortage of "one-on-one" time that our busy lifestyles seem to generate, bedtimes in many homes have evolved into something more uncomfortable than comforting.

Younger children sometimes perceive bedtime as separation: from parents, from group activities, from light, and even human contact itself. The fact that civilization is usually no farther away than the very next room makes no difference at all. It is a confusing and uncertain world outside of our families, and without the security that comes from the mere physical presence of each member, anything can happen. And sometimes does.

The most common method of dealing with "bedtime blues"

is to have a routine. It really doesn't matter what—they vary from house to house. The important outcome is a secondary sense of security that comes from knowing what to expect. So, whether it's:

> * story, night-light, close the closet (check first for intruders); or
>
> * brush teeth, nursery rhymes, tickle games, bedtime prayers, close the closet (check first for intruders—human or alien, it could be either one); or
>
> * bed-snack, brush teeth, drink of water, read a book, check under the bed for black holes or any toys that might have mutated into monsters while you were busy brushing teeth...

A routine is a safeguard against all manner of murder and mayhem, even if it's only temporary. It is a talisman against the forces of evil that run rampant in today's world. And if you think this perspective is a little over-exaggerated, you're absolutely right. Because in the world of four feet and under, everything is exaggerated.

Some families have opted for a strong dose of reality therapy. They are very open with their children and consistently reinforce their own adamant belief that there is nothing to be afraid of because most of what frightens kids these days is "just pretend." Their children will agree and even parrot the phrase themselves when confronted with something frightening or unnerving. But at night, it's a different story. Pretend might be insignificant to adults but it is paramount to children. Besides, you didn't say there was no such thing as pretend—you said, "Just pretend." Big difference.

Some parents get frustrated and often angry at a child's inability to deal with the concept, or to trust their parents enough to protect them even if they can't deal with it. Some react with shame or embarrassment that their own children are such cowards, or feel resentment toward the child for the time that dealing with the problem every night takes away from their own relaxation.

Added to the threat of physical safety, this undermining of the relationship that comes from constant conflict over the matter between parent and child causes an excessive need for attention. Which, in turn, causes the unreasonable demands for one more drink, one more kiss, one more of anything they can think of. Including medicine, should they feel a sore throat coming on. The truth is, if you have one of those children who have a difficult time going to bed each night, you might be hanging on to the last hope that most parents have in your situation: that they will someday simply grow out of it.

In the old days, we used to refer to such problems as "stages." It's where that hopeful philosophy that whatever the trouble was, the child would "grow out of it" came from. Which actually wasn't far wrong. Children do go through stages (or phases) of growth, just like everything else in the cycle of life. That's why—especially in cases like these—it becomes vitally important to take a closer look at the stages.

From birth to the age of five, a child goes through more physical changes than any other time in life. Mental growth during this "stage" concerns itself mostly with physical knowledge. Such as how high to lift the feet each time to successfully walk upstairs; the rate at which liquid flows out of a glass while pouring it into another; and the practice of small motor skills like buttoning, tying, zipping and snapping.

For a four-year-old to make a peanut butter and jelly sandwich without tearing a hole in the bread during the spreading part is a major accomplishment. It takes lots of practice. On the other hand, a ten-year-old who has never made his own sandwich will successfully achieve the task in one try with a few verbal instructions. That's because he has already mastered the necessary skills in other ways and has the ability to transfer that experience to the new situation. He is at a different level. A different stage. To expect the same level of performance out of the four-year-old is asking the impossible. Yet, when it comes to mental tasks, we often do.

Most of us would not dream of insisting that our preschooler practice plunking a basketball into a standard-size hoop, simply because—unless you have given birth to a human dynamo—it is physically impossible for them to do. On the other hand, many parents can be found trying to make a toddler look behind a chair for a ball that rolled under (as opposed to fussing and crying about it) when the child has not yet advanced beyond the "out of sight is gone" stage. The same is true with pretend.

A popular example of this that psychologists like to cite is the experiment where a large box is placed in a room of preschoolers. An adult tells them they are not to open the box, or even look into it, because there is a tiger inside. Then the adult leaves the room. A hidden camera shows some talking, giggling, and an occasional brave soul who will get out of their seat to actually touch the box. But nobody opens it.

The Nature Of Children

After a while, the adult returns and tells everyone it was only a game, and they were only pretending there was a tiger. To prove this, he opens the box and shows each child that it is empty. Everyone laughs and enjoys the joke. The adult closes the box and leaves the room again. Same scenario as before. On return, he asks why no one opened the box. General consensus? Because there was a tiger inside.

You could not pull this on an eight-year-old. But the little ones don't just believe anything they're told, they believe everything. Not because they are cowards: children by nature are very brave. It's because they have simply not developed their deductive reasoning skills beyond the physical level, yet. And looking back on the human race as a whole, up until about fifty years ago, they didn't need to.

It has only been since our recent emersion of our young into adult worlds that the sort of demands we make on children these days was even dreamed of. In our triumph of no longer having to be subject to the rising and setting of the sun—or even the seasons—to survive, we have also given up the sense of peace and security that the very constancy those things carried with them. Of course those things aren't really lost. It's just that we have opted to live in our own self-made environments, now, where one can have light at any time on even the darkest night, and fresh vegetables are always in season.

The only drawback to this switch is that we seem to have left human nature back in the Stone Age. Not that we've denied it: the thing about human nature is you can't deny it. A lot of well-meaning people have had breakdowns by trying to.

So, what is the answer? A new "back to nature" movement

to recapture our sense of peace and security? Of course not. But the problem is we haven't made a place for nature in our new societies, yet. All new things need adjustments and lifestyles are no different. But in the meantime (it always takes a couple generations to make any major changes in the race—look how long feudalism held on) we've got some pretty confused people running around out there.

Let's get back to bedtime. If it's true that a young child cannot possibly go beyond the developmental level he is in, no matter how clever or skilled he is, how are we supposed to make the sort of connection that is needed in order to deal with such a major problem? And it is major. Anything that consistently disrupts your peace, your relationships, and your sense of self-confidence is major. No matter how many others are going through the same thing.

All babies are born the same way, too, but not one of us can exchange the experience for someone else's. Birthing children, like many other life experiences, is one where in spite of all the help and comfort available from others, you—and you, alone—have to deal with it.

All right, so how do we deal? You start by making a decision to quit insisting that your children rise up to your level of expectations, and instead, "bend down" to theirs. You just pretend. If they cannot meet you in your world, then visit them in theirs. It isn't hard because in that world, you are already a hero. What's more, it may be the only time and circumstance you will be offered in your life to play this role, so, don't pass up the chance. Because what you do there will be very real. Remember, it might just be play-acting for you but it will be

The Nature Of Children

amazingly and significantly real for your children.

> **Children believe everything..**

In this first stage of childhood, children believe everything. So, if you tell them there are no such thing as ghosts, they will believe you and agree. But they will also believe that there are. And you would probably be more shocked than they would if one showed up in the closet while you were checking it because they knew one was in there all along. They believe everything.

The point is, if they have ghosts in their world, teach them how to deal with ghosts, even if it takes a little pretending. Try, "You are braver than any ghost because you are a (whatever your last name is) and ghosts have been afraid of us for thousands of years. Why do you think they hide in closets? Get out of there, ghost!" Now, here's where your hero stuff comes in. Open the closet and say, "See that? Ran away completely! Ghosts are so afraid of our family that if your baby sister crawled over here and opened the closet, they'd run away from her, too. That's just the way it is."

Then get on with the bedtime story. And if you have to literally create your own genealogy of "brave relations" in order to substantiate this claim, then do it. Remember, you are in the world of pretend; you can make or create anything you want to here. So, make it count.

Why should you bother? Because even as childhood fears carry over into everyday life, (and if they are having a disruptive effect on your everyday life, they have) so do attitudes of bravery or honesty, or any other virtue you might want to promote. In fact, this is the only place you have the power to bring this about. So, think about it. If your children are missing something about bedtime, maybe you've been missing something, too. In the meantime, here are a few ways to turn those bedtimes into better times:

LIMIT VIEWING. Children that are easily frightened are often more sensitive than others. A cartoon that has no effect on most kids might be subtly disturbing to the overly sensitive ones. These children do better when focused on the more positive, concrete issues in life. If it's a choice between *Power Rangers* who are defending the universe against evil, or *Arthur*, who is in a dilemma about his science project... pick Arthur.

AVOID THREATENING ROOM DÉCOR. Posters of the latest space movie might be momentarily desirable (because others are doing it) but at night and alone, things like this take on a whole new perspective.

EXTEND BEDTIME ROUTINES. Exchange those extra drinks of water and more Kleenex for more one-on-one time with your kids. But make it a "joint effort." Make a deal. If they will try harder at bedtime, then give them extra time at the beginning and not the end of the bedtime hour. If eight o'clock is the limit, start at seven-thirty. If it's important enough to them, they will choose to sacrifice some of their time in order to extend yours. If they fool around and miss their special appointment, you can be sympathetic without being the bad guy, since it was their choice and not yours.

AVOID EMOTIONAL TOPICS. Bedtime, like mealtime, is a safe zone. Bringing up arguments or previous bad conduct should never disrupt it.

MAKE "BEFORE BEDTIME" ACTIVITIES "WIND DOWN" ACTIVITIES. All of us need time to unwind, even children. If your children have a hard time calming down before bed, don't allow activities (such as wrestling) that stir up the adrenaline just before bedtime. Allow for a little quiet time before the bedtime hour.

KEEP BEDTIMES CONSISTENT. Children who are on a schedule are much easier to maintain than children who aren't. A child who goes to bed at eight-thirty every night and is out late visiting for a special occasion, will probably fall asleep before arriving home. In the same way, a consistent bedtime will trigger the child's physical clock at home, too, and they will consistently become sleepy at bedtime.

AVOID SUGAR AND CAFINE AS A BED-SNACK: they don't call these things high energy foods for nothing.

GIVE A FIVE-MINUTE WARNING. It's hard to "switch gears" if you're in the middle of something, especially if you're a kid. A simple "five minutes to bedtime," notification gives them time to wrap up whatever they're doing and avoid arguments about what time it really is.

HAVE A "PLAN B." If activities outside the home make bedtime too late for the routine, have a second bedtime routine for these very occasions. Shorter, of course. But make it include something (such as a special rhyme or song, or "butterfly kiss") that you only do at these times, and that they are expecting beforehand. That way there won't be any crushed psyches for having skipped the all-important routine.

Bedtimes can be the best part of the day, or the worst, depending on you. But with a little extra effort to wield the "magic of pretend," it really is possible to change a "bedtime blues baby" to a happy one, before they have to grow out of it. Simply start with a decision to change. But be careful. There is an old legend about a terrible ogre who fell in love with a beautiful princess who would not allow anything that wasn't good approach her. So, he put on a mask and pretended to be good until he won her. After they were married, he discovered that he could not get the mask off—it had become part of his face—and he had become good.

There really is no such thing as pretend.

31

Back to School Blues

There are many children who do not look forward to going back to school in September. All for various reasons. For some, being excited about school is simply, "Not cool." For others, it means a necessary return to the work and routine of real life. Summers offer a door into that "anything could happen" realm, and at the very least, a welcome respite from the all too necessary world that a school year represents. But for some kids, going back to school takes a tremendous act of courage on the part of the student: and sometimes their parents, as well.

Though only a small percentage of today's schools fall into the category of being the next volatile hotbed for mass destruction, an alarming number of them do not live up to the standard of being a safe haven for children. The times are to blame, mostly. Because we are living in an age when the freedom of the individual has taken precedence over the freedom of the group.

Mixed with a general lack of discipline by teachers and administrators, what was once a place of higher learning has turned into a learning ground for a different kind of education altogether. Very little of which is actually filtered through academic sources. True, the majority of children who graduate from today's programs will come away with the basic knowledge of reading, writing and arithmetic. Hopefully.

But have you ever noticed how many of our teen and young adult citizens who have jobs as cashiers, have trouble making change when the register doesn't tell them exactly how? Say, for instance giving them a ten dollar bill and a quarter when the total was five sixteen, simply because you didn't want eighty-four cents jingling around in your pocket for the rest of the day. It can be a shocking experience. Especially when you realize that you could very well be having this transaction with the future president of a bank.

Does this mean kids are getting dumber and dumber?

Absolutely not. Is it due to overcrowding, or the lack of nutrition in overly processed foods? Not enough to have significant impact on this particular problem, even though more than a few industries and organizations would like you to think so. There are three things lacking in today's school environment (including private schools) that are necessary to success in education. They are: ***discipline***, ***academic content***, and ***enthusiasm***. The most important of which is enthusiasm. But it is impossible to have sufficient enthusiasm in the midst of chaos, or without anything to specifically be enthusiastic about.

There are an amazing number of educators in our modern system that single-handedly forge these things out in their own individual classrooms, and—if the truth be known—they are probably the ones responsible for holding the entire out-dated and inefficient system together for so long. They are the teachers parents pass the word about to others in the community: the ones your child has to have at least two or three of in their entire twelve years of school in order to not only survive the system, but to come out with something of value when they are through.

An amazing percentage of what these individuals teach cannot only be remembered—but quoted—many years later. Usually along with an appreciative mention of a specific teacher's name in the process. Children never forget what is truly important... because they're so impressionable.

That's human nature.

The majority of today's kids will survive these statistics, and go on to further their own education and live fairly productive lives throughout adulthood. But for those who find themselves on the fringes, school can be traumatic in many ways. To be a "fringe-dweller" does not necessarily mean one has a learning disorder—because most of them don't.

Instead, they are the ones who tend to have too much of something. Too much shyness, too much boastfulness, too much brains or too much ignorance, or even too much beauty or homeliness. Too mean, or too kind. Too much of anything puts a child outside that illusive circle of acceptance we call "normal." And if one has ever been disdainful of society's class systems, let it be mentioned here that children can be more ruthless than adults when it comes to classifying.

Nowadays it is the peers who seem to hold the biggest sway in schools. And even if your child is a model individual at home, you would be surprised how easily they can—and do—slip into the attitudes and behaviors of whatever is acceptable at school. Their use of language even changes. Which is a good thing for the most part, because without this amazing adaptability, they would tend to be crushed under the pressures that circulate there. But that doesn't solve the long-term problems of attaining a better education. Problems which are beginning to find their way into national concerns as well as individual homes. Everyone knows there are problems. But as a parent, what specifically can you do about them?

Here are a few things that will help:

BE ENTHUSIASTIC. First and foremost. Sure, there are problems at school, but it does not help to constantly berate those things if you can't do anything about them. Enthusiasm can actually override a multitude of problems. If you can't find anything to be excited about, then at least give your child a chance to have a positive experience by making a pact with yourself not to say anything negative about it. Maybe even try saying, "Oh, boy, school!" every once in a while, even if the only wonderful thing you can relate to is the smell of a newly-sharpened pencil.

BE ATTENTIVE. Children are constantly giving out signals. Make it a point to notice whether your child has had a good day or a bad one, and find out why. Many things that happen in school are beyond verbal communication for children. Perhaps they were embarrassed about not knowing an answer when called on, felt uncomfortable for a long time afterward but didn't know why. They might even start worrying about being called on, again. Most children have had this experience at one time or another, and most will not even mention it when they get home. But those who have suffered traumatic proportions over it will only get "back on track" when outside adjustments are made by parents or teachers. Things like extra help with homework, or positive reinforcement for better listening will help them overcome the experience rather than allowing them to assume they are simply not as smart as everyone else.

MAKE CORRECTIONS. Never let an incident or inappropriate attitude by without pointing out the right way to your children. Then go one step further and help them make things right. The world can look pretty confusing from a child's perspective, and—contrary to popular opinion—children are not born with an automatic propensity for wisdom. Teach them early how to fix their mistakes, and you will also be lightening their burdens in the future.

> *Teach them early how to fix their mistakes, and you will also be lightening their burdens in the future..*

BE CAREFUL WITH FEELINGS. If your child tells you, "I hate school!" try to avoid answers like, "You can't hate school. You have to go to school, so, that's that." To tell them they can't feel a certain thing after they already do makes them think something must be wrong with them, personally. You can get the same point across by saying instead, "I'm sorry you feel that way. We really don't have any choice about going to school but maybe we could think of some ways to make it better for you." Then think of some.

DON'T PROJECT YOUR OWN ACADEMIC WEAKNESSES ONTO YOUR CHILDREN. If your child comes to you with a homework problem, don't give them a response of, "I never could get it right when I was your age, either. Must run in the family." Remember, children believe what you tell them. And if you tell them it runs in the family, it will just add to the original problem. Even if it's true, and the subject still baffles you, send them to the other parent (or friend, or family member) with the suggestion, "Why don't you ask, your dad? He's great at that subject." Then they won't have to worry about what might be "running in their family" before it ever really shows up. And maybe it never will. Children have a tendency to take on the strengths of both their parents more than the weaknesses. That's human nature.

FIND OUT WHAT'S IMPORTANT. Not only according to the teacher and the school but to your children, as well. Do they need another parent on a field trip and your child has impulsively "volunteered" you when you absolutely hate that sort of thing? Try to do at least one of those things every year, anyway. Not so much for the teacher (even though any extra adult on a field trip is appreciated) but for what it means to your child. Do they want to participate in an extracurricular activity and all you can see is one more commitment during an already hectic week, not to mention the money? Sit down together and look over all the "pros and cons" before you make a hasty decision.

BE PROTECTIVE. Are you uncomfortable letting your first grader ride the bus, or your teenage daughter walk home alone from school? Don't deny the basic instincts of parenthood. Take them yourself, or make arrangements for them to go with others as opposed to trying to believe that such experiences will "make them more independent." Webster's dictionary defines independence with the words: "to have no allegiance with or dependence on anything or anybody." The only people who benefit from that situation are hardened criminals. The fact that most of the world's population lives in cities, interacting every day with others, proves that we humans don't really want to be that way, either. So, go with your instincts.

School is a necessary part of growing up and a necessary part of becoming a productive citizen in today's world. But like everything else in life, there are good things and bad things about it. And like everything else in life, it's pretty much up to the individual whether it ends up being a good experience or a bad one. The attitudes, encouragement, and enthusiasm of a parent can make all the difference in helping a child choose which one of those it will be for them. A wise parent can actually help their children choose the best. And when a child chooses to make the best of school...

Then it doesn't leave much room for the back-to-school blues.

32

Bored With It All

Parents are often dismayed at the frequent complaints of, "I'm bored," from children who seem to have more than they need to keep them occupied until adulthood. They wonder how this can be. Or if their children are somehow missing some connection as to what all the interesting things in their room will do. Mixed with the feelings of guilt parents sometimes experience at having to spend so much time away from their children in order to make a living, these two conditions can have some perplexing results.

The topic is one of the most widely discussed between parents and educators and there are many suggestions for solutions to choose from. They are "band-aid solutions" mostly: a wide variety of temporary fixes that will hold until the child moves into another stage. Or at least until another band-aid solution can be applied. And if it seems like the price of band-aids are going up lately, they are. So, what's a parent to

The Nature Of Children

do? Most just settle for the best they can, which usually ends up trickling down to where the child is faced with the same option...

They do the best they can.

Considering a child must always make do with whatever is at hand, it is no wonder they are often bored. Couple this with the fact that children have more energy than they actually need or use these days and you get a rather volatile force with very few positive outlets. Results? A real danger zone for misconduct and negative behaviors. But before we can come to a more workable solution, let's take a closer look at what boredom really is.

First of all, it is a lack of the right kind of stimulation. Just as there are certain vitamins and nutrients essential to the well-being of humans, there are also certain mental and physical needs that are just as important for a well-balanced individual. No matter how old they are. And as much as we think we are being sufficiently stimulated by today's popular pastimes like television and video games, there is surprisingly little real stimulation going on with those pastimes, at all.

> *The brain is a mighty wonder.*

The brain is a mighty wonder. It has a way of switching off all other demands from the body as long as attention is sufficiently held. Which is a unique process for intense projects but can be highly detrimental if sustained over long periods of time. And we're not talking hours, here. We're talking days, weeks, months, and even years of the majority of our time.

Since the majority of us participate in some if not most of this lifestyle, we tend to put those long-term consequences out of our mind in much the same way as those other things we rarely mention or talk about. Like growing old, or the earth's dwindling resources, or what the future might bring beyond the next few years. Once again, because most families are having the same experiences, we tend to think it must be normal. Which, luckily, has absolutely no effect on human nature, at all.

Society has gone through many changes over the millennia but humans have not. An interesting testimony to this is the amazing physical abilities our athletes are able to attain by simply using what they have even though most of the rest of us are content to sit at home and remain out of shape. It has even been said that the more energy they expend, the more energetic they feel. Which is why going to the gym tends to refresh people as opposed to wearing them out. Unless it's only a once-a-year deal.

The brain works in the same way. Its capabilities are "on tap" until used, and can never be all used up, which is a wonder by itself. At the same time, it is in complete subjection to its owner and will not release this wonderful ability unless sufficiently called upon. Nor does it complain if it never is. Most of us live through our entire lives without using much more than about three percent of its potential. But we don't worry too much about it because we all think that's normal. It also makes us tend to forget we have these wonderful resources at hand. But they can be a gold mine for parents with children faced with boredom.

Here are some tried and true ways to tap into them:

TRY SOMETHING NEW. Though children have an amazing capacity to watch the same movies, play the same games, and eat the same meals, there is always a feeling of adventure when anything new comes on the scene. Those who tend to shy away from new things can usually be won over by a parent or sibling's enthusiasm and the encouragement that they just might discover a new favorite.

EXPAND YOUR OWN IDEAS of what being actively involved really is. A child does not merely always want to be entertained; many times he doesn't want to. Instead he would rather participate in something of value that he sees you busy with, such as meal preparation or a household project. Many chores that are tedious for adults can be challenging and fun for children. But remember: children mirror our attitudes: if you act like such duties are pure drudgery, so will they.

TAKE UP A FAMILY QUEST. Instead of just doing something for a day or on the spur of a moment, pick a long-term family activity that everyone can take part in. Such as bird watching or rock collecting. And delve a little deeper into the subject than simply seeing how many birds you can count in the backyard or how many rocks you can gather. The library is full of wonderful resources on how and where to look for these things, and there are even clubs you can join to go on outings. Or learn another language together. It doesn't really matter what you choose because you have the added benefit of it being doubly potent simply because your children are doing this activity with you. Something that takes

259

precedence over an individual activity, every time.

SEEK OUT THEIR TALENTS. Do you have a junior Einstein on your hands if only he had his own laboratory? It can be wonderful fun for the whole family to set up a home laboratory and do research. This not only beats a game, it can have long-term effects on school and even career choices, later on. Do you have a girl who's convinced she's the next *National Velvet* if only she had a horse to ride to find out? You don't have to live in the country and raise livestock to let her try. There are many places that offer this kind of activity for an afternoon for less than the price of a pizza. So, let her try. She may decide to go into bicycle racing the next week but that's okay, too.

START A FAMILY READING CLUB with contests, prizes, and goals. Have a once a week library night during the contest time and read at least one book out-loud as a group. Have them tell or act out scenes (for the extraverts in your family) from their individual reading times that they can share with others, and finish with a "Grand Finale" of a celebration on prize night. Remember, these activities do not have to be extravagant. A build-your-own-sundae and a paperback copy of an interesting book can be worth ten times more, just because it's a celebration.

LEARN SOMETHING of the history of your town or your state and then go "exploring" on Saturdays.

LOOK FOR THE STARS. A "starry-eyed" child beats a

moody one for company every time. So, find out what it is that "puts stars" into the eyes of your children, then make it a point to provide ways for them to learn more, become more and dream more about it. You'll never be sorry you did.

If you look at boredom as a signal that little brains have been "too long on the charger" without being used enough instead of trying to find another way to occupy them, again, the results will be better for everybody. And try looking farther than the next room. Robert Louis Stevenson once wrote:

> *"The world is so full*
> *Of a number of things,*
> *I'm sure we should all*
> *Be as happy as kings."*

And he was right. The world is big, with more than enough things to interest everybody for longer than any of us could ever live to discover it all. With a little practice at exploration and observation, it won't take any time at all before you and your family find yourselves in a wonderful place.

Where it is no longer possible to be bored with it all.

33

Undercover Summers

Summers are for relaxing. Time to take a break from all those mundane schedules of the school year and do absolutely nothing. Or, simply play. Some kids think summer means sleeping in, staying up late, and long hours of uninterrupted time with friends. For others, it means summer camps, family vacations, and extended stays with far-off cousins that are more fun than anyone to be with. But for all children everywhere, the most popular characteristic of summer can be summed up in two words:

No School.

Parents tend to look at summers in a different light. What to do with the kids during the hours you are working? Which summer camps to send them to and which local daytime programs are not already filled to capacity. How much you can really afford this year for those special interest activities like drama clubs, sports camps, or karate lessons? Summertime can be stress-times for parents who are already stretched to the limits in so many other ways. But one of the most frequently asked questions from all parents is: what about academics?

Should I send my children to summer school? Should I keep them "brushed up" on math and reading skills so they will not forget everything they learned and have to start out behind everyone else next fall? Billy got a borderline passing grade in English—should I hire a tutor? And what about those learning centers you're always hearing about over the radio and TV, where they claim they can "raise your child's grade level" if you follow their program and even your children will be happier?

All good ideas. But what do you do if your children aren't interested in any of those? More important, what do you do if they are but you simply can't swing it financially at this time? Outside of vacation Bible schools (which are still free to the general public), most extra-curricular activities tend to get pretty expensive. Which leaves the greater portion of summer vacationers with way too much idle time on their hands. Not to mention a bit rusty in the academic department. What's more, any suggested activities that even remotely resemble schoolwork are usually met with disdain by children who have made it their personal quest to goof off for the whole season. Almost as a matter of pride.

That's when it's time for parents to do a little "undercover work." Because the truth is, kids do tend to get rusty on academics if they do nothing to stimulate thinking during the summer. Leaving the thinking part of the brain un-stimulated for long periods usually constitutes nothing less than a jump-start to get it going again later on in the fall. The definition of jump-start meaning a tremendous jolt of power to transfer energy. Which is not always pleasant. At either end. Simply because it drains the source and shocks the recipient. But how to go about all this without ruining the spirit of summer?

First of all, don't always let them know when you're doing it. And before you get any twinges of behaving sneaky or unethical, let's clarify the perspective here. This kind of anonymity falls more under the category of doing good deeds without having to have them connected to your name up in lights for having done them. Such people in most societies are referred to as saints. Especially when the outcome is for the benefit of all. Coupled with the fact that children are great for catching anything out of the ordinary, you will automatically have their interest. What's Mom up to, anyway? What's Dad doing out there in the garage? Everybody loves a mystery.

Most children can be easily coerced to try something different, especially if it's challenging. That is, unless it's a food item: the reputation of which has been tainted by too many parents who have handed over a plate of artichokes and promised their unwary offspring that if they try it, they'll like it. Working undercover in the academic department is actually much easier than in the field of nutrition. It just takes a little pre-planning.

Following are a few suggestions to make that planning easier:

> **TEAM UP WITH FRIENDS AND NEIGHBORS.** You're not alone! Not only does anyone with kids usually have the same struggles and questions as you, a group can always come up with a greater array of answers and ideas to combat them. There are also other benefits. Children get

more enjoyment out of activities they can interact with others in; and parents who are pressed for time can still provide the best of these activities with their children by sharing the supervision with other parents. There's strength in numbers.

SURPRISE THEM BY STEPPING OUT OF YOUR WORLD. Children have amazing powers of perception, and often know us better than we do. If you love reading and your idea of a fun time is a trip to the library, the declaration that during summer they will get to visit that wonderful place at least once a week is not going to be much of a surprise. However, if you check out a book on entomology and call them out to the garage in order to construct a habitat in which they will be able to collect and study bugs for the summer... science begins to take on a whole new meaning.

MAKE YOUR HOME A HUB. Uncomfortable about where and with whom your children will be playing this summer? Start building a rocket in your backyard. You do not have to be a NASA expert in order to do this. It doesn't even have to have an engine or the capacity to actually blast off. And if your end result turns out to look more like the north blockade of Fort Laramie instead of a spacecraft when you're through, it really doesn't matter. If it's something kids can work on and crawl through, your children will stay busy at it for weeks. So will half the rest of the neighborhood.

The same holds true for a clubhouse, a miniature golf course, or anything else you can come up with that they will have to build on their own. **Note**: don't be cheap on materials, here. Remember, children need fodder for their brains. Make sure they are supplied with plenty of things to work with, as well as pictures and directions to follow in order to succeed. It is also helpful to put an end to the project along with summer, (or before, if interest wanes), so they can overcome their natural propensity to leave messes after the fun is over.

READ FOR MONEY. Uh-oh, is this a bribe? You bet it is. But there are times when nothing less than a bribe will do, and this is one of them. The thing about a bribe is, the person who is offering it is usually banking on something much bigger and more valuable in return. Same with reading for money. If you offer your children a dollar per book (not to include picture books or toddler series if your child is of legitimate school age) it is going to seem to them like they just struck the "Mother lode." How dumb can you get? Why they could read all kinds of books this summer. Man—you are going to be coming to them just to take out a loan they're going to read so many books!

> *A book can educate a child like no other medium can achieve.*

Which is exactly what you want. Because each time they read a single book, they will be touched, enlightened, thought-provoked, and literally hooked on books. A book can educate a child like no other medium can achieve. This method has never failed, in one summer, to produce children that are devoted readers for a lifetime. That in itself, is priceless.

CREATE A VACATION ATMOSPHERE. One family who had three boys decided that during summer, the children would not have to make beds, take baths, or wear clothes until school started, again. They didn't even insist that they eat regular meals. Sound a little too far out? They did this by letting them sleep in sleeping bags instead of their beds, go swimming as many times as they wanted every day in the backyard pool, and not have to wear anything but bathing suits unless they went out in public. The center of the kitchen table was set with a constant supply of peanut butter, jelly and bread so they could make their own sandwiches any time they felt the need. The results? The boys thought it was one of the best summer vacations they ever had. Total freedom.

DELEGATE RESPONSIBILITY. Many parents dread the coming of summer simply for the extra work it brings. More activities, more kids running through the house, extended bedtimes, etc. But it doesn't have to be that way. Children will not only rise to the challenge of responsibility, they will excel in it. Give them the opportunity to clean the house if they are going to have friends over (before you say, "Yeah, right," let's clarify giving them the opportunity: "When you get the house clean, you may have your friends over." Big difference.)

Better yet, give them an opportunity to earn money from extra chores. There's always a need for more money during the summer. If some of your children's activities can be paid for by their own earnings, they won't be so quick to pester you over things you have no intentions of giving in to. Like a super-slime sleep-over party. If they want one that bad, let them foot the bill and clean up afterward. You might be surprised at how practical your own children turn out to be.

Think some of these things aren't "academic" enough? Think again. Anything that promotes independent working skills, cooperation with others, deductive reasoning, and the ability to look at something from a different perspective, is a brain stimulator. Learning need not always entail drudgery. Any parent can be an undercover summer agent. Your mission —should you choose to accept it—is to make your children think they are taking a break from learning, when in fact, they are really learning more. Not only more but better.

Which of us cannot remember best those nostalgic summers of our youth? The warm fragrant air of an outside evening, friendships that are bonded by a seal one never forgets... and most of all, that ultimate contentment of being totally free and unencumbered for weeks on end. Summers tend to be the most impressionable times of childhood. They are also a rare opportunity for parents to impress their children in the very best of ways. And you can do it.

By making it an "undercover summer."

34

Going to Extremes

Some of the most horrendous experiences in life—for parents and children—can be attributed to the family vacation. It tends to be a time of extremes. For children, they often find themselves extremely crowded, extremely hot, extremely wet, extremely tired, extremely hungry, or maybe even extremely weird. Like having to sleep in the same tent with an aunt you never met, who not only snores but shaves.

For parents, it's usually a case of having forgotten something important that snowballs into nightmare proportions. Like the fact that Sally gets carsick on long winding roads, and her brother Ben has a sensitive nose. Or how quickly disasters can occur, and how utterly useless leftover napkins from a fast-food-stop are for cleaning up major messes. And how different places can look in a travel brochure, as opposed to being there. One can never feel the heat or see the bugs in any of these advertisements for the ultimate outdoor experience.

What's more, family vacations seem to be just far enough apart and offer such unlimited variations, that one can consistently be caught off guard no matter how much planning and organization goes into them. But there is a word for this. A very good word that is part of what keeps drawing us back again and again, and keeps us looking for the ultimate vacation experience. That word is adventure. Everyone craves adventure. Even the quietest and meekest of us have some deep down craving for it because it's part of human nature. It can be satisfied in many different ways.

Some people are content with doing the same thing every year, which greatly cuts down on the unexpected mishap factor. Others aren't so easily satisfied but are great at looking ahead and preparing in advance for all manner of possibilities. They are the ones who always bring extra, "just in case." Then there are those who simply get an idea and go for it. Although there are numerous ways of taking a vacation, the main goal of all methods is generally to relax and have fun.

Which is why parents are often baffled when children—who should be having a wonderful time with all this relaxing and funning—get notoriously cranky, whiney, or even downright naughty. Which can turn the best of times into the worst of times, no matter where you happen to be. The truth is, the problem usually lies in the destination. Not the physical one, though the symptoms are physical, which tends to throw people off. Instead of going to a campground, or a resort, or even Aunt Nettie's farm for a family reunion, people often end up taking their children to the absolute worst place they could ever go.

Which is to extremes.

While children are the best enthusiasts, they are also the most limited members of the group when it comes to the family vacation. That's because they are the only members who are still expending most of their energy on growth and development, and therefore, have little or no reserves when it comes to stretching their limits. What's more, they don't have much experience at recognizing the symptoms of getting "low on fuel" and usually hit empty before they even think of pulling over... leaving themselves prime targets for others who are still speeding down the road. To be "hit from behind" when you least expect it tends to make anyone cranky, or whiney, or even downright naughty. Nobody likes getting knocked on their ear. And it is quite impossible to "have a little more patience" or "wait just a little longer" when you have absolutely no patience or wait left in your tank.

The answer to this dilemma is to be aware of the unique limitations of children. It's important to realize that they have nothing in common with personality and willpower. Which is why "What were you thinking?" or "Can't you wait even..." so often fails to obtain results in these surroundings. Even more important, it becomes vital for parents to make a habit of "running point" for their kids, in order to ward off any unexpected attacks.

That's because it takes an experienced eye to recognize an accident waiting to happen, and experience is what children have the least of. If you can remember that the greater portion of everything they do is a first time deal, it will go a long way toward helping you dole out a little extra "patience and wait" from your own reserves to help them compensate.

Here are several valuable tips to help keep your children from going to extremes:

TAKE MORE THAN ENOUGH. Being on vacation—especially outdoors—is extremely stimulating. Kids tend to eat more, expend more energy and sleep harder than they usually do at home. So, plan for extra, even though you know "Jenny never eats more than..." Better to have some left over than not enough to go around.

ALWAYS HAVE A "PLAN B." Things often don't work out the way they should on a vacation. If your canoe trip happens to land you on a river that is running low this year, with little more than inches of water on most of the runs, change the main activities to swimming, sunning, and sightseeing. Shorter canoe runs are better than hauling, slogging, and sloshing watercraft and cranky children in sweltering heat over sand and rock bars for hours, simply to say you've done what you set out to do.

BE VERSATILE. Were you planning an old-fashioned cook-out over an open fire but it turned eight o'clock before you gathered enough wood and got the thing going sufficiently hot enough to cook anything? Don't make the kids wait until nine to finally get their dinner. Break out the reliable old camp stove and quick food. Save that nostalgic culinary experience you've been thinking about for the next day: when you can start the fire around four, in order to get a meal done by six. That's the way they used to do it in the "old days," anyway.

AVOID STRESS OVERLOADS. Does Jimmy have a hard time sitting still for long periods? Then don't expect him to be any different just because you're headed for

Disneyland. Make a few extra bathroom stops, let him get out and help when you're refueling, and give him things to occupy his mind like watching the map and looking for road signs. It also helps to give him a little incentive to behave "until the next stop" by rewarding him with an occasional treat when he makes it. Not necessarily food. It could be anything from a video game at a truck stop, to a little extra pocket change for that souvenir he's looking forward to.

FOLLOW YOUR INSTINCTS. Has Uncle Howard promised to do all the cooking but he can't manage to get breakfast on until ten when your darlings are up and running at seven? Bring along "emergency rations" for situations like this. It will save everyone's patience in the long run. Most children don't drool over Denver Omelets, anyway. The same goes for activities. Has everyone voted to ride some colossus roller-coaster and you know Kathy is secretly afraid of heights? Then help her out of the situation by suggesting an alternate activity without making her admit to the entire crowd why she would rather not. Even if it means telling them you're not terribly excited about heights, and maybe Kathy could "tear herself away" long enough to accompany you on...

USE CHILD PROTECTION DEVICES. Got a friend or family member who seems to take pleasure in criticizing everything the children do? Run some interference. Notice one of your kids is sitting off to themselves and not participating? Find out why. Children are often bewildered at feelings of inadequacy during group activities, or embarrassment in public restrooms, and all manner of other adjustments to communal life that others seem to take in their stride. This is a good time to explain things and reaffirm your acceptance of them for just who they are. No matter how they feel.

TOUCH BASES WITH THE CHILD YOU WERE. Be tolerant of those less than perfect efforts—or lack of them—and remember what it was like to feel the warm excitement of playing late into a summer evening. How important the little things were, like roasting one more marshmallow to perfection even though you've eaten enough to make you sick, already. To stay a bit later for one last ride, or one last dive into the hotel pool. Or to be awakened in time to see the fireworks even though you accidentally fell asleep beforehand. Like you, your children will never forget it.

> *The most important element in any family vacation is the family.*

The family vacation can be a "heads or tails," "win or lose" situation, even if you have all the money in the world to play with. That's because the most important element in any family vacation is the family. Relationships can be strengthened or weakened during these times, but, as with much of parenting, it is the parents who hold the upper hand.

Children rarely go to extremes by themselves, but are usually taken there—quite unexpectedly—by someone else. That's because it's their nature to go along with practically anything. A parent who recognizes this beforehand and makes an effort to steer them clear of disasters, will receive something much more valuable than whatever extra effort they put out to accomplish it. They will get a more memorable family vacation — an adventure — for the whole family. At the same time, they will impart that wonderful sense of security that can only come from a parent who has successfully protected their children...

From going to extremes.

Forever

35

Touching Bases

Everyone needs to be touched. It is the most basic of human needs and one that—if neglected—leads to a lack of caring and understanding for others. Working parents and modern conveniences have promoted a wide-spread shortage of this in our society. Inventions such as the car, the microwave, and the television have made it possible for a child to be raised in virtual isolation even though surrounded by people.

Association is not contact. Yet, many of the families who have become nothing more than an association of people living in the same house would be startled to have this pointed out to them. In fact, most of them are caring parents who are doing their best to provide for their children in every way they know how. But in spite of this, their home-life seems to suffer from the chronic symptoms of bickering, disorder, and a lack of enthusiasm for anything other than immediate personal gratification.

The same mother who props a bottle in an infant's crib at feeding time because she has to get ready for work, will do it again in a stroller at a mall, simply because she wants to shop.

After a while, it will become the preferred mode of feeding because the child seems happy with it and there are always more things to do than there is time in a day.

On the other hand, some children are born with the type of personality that demands attention. They have no problem with interrupting or jumping onto a parent's lap no matter what the adults are involved in. They will not go without the necessary attention they crave even if it can only be had by getting themselves in trouble.

Then there are the quiet ones. They rarely get out of line or in trouble and are often overlooked in the hustle and bustle of things. Because of this, they are sometimes perceived as needing less attention, when in fact, they need more. These children tend to actually be more sensitive because they usually consider the wants and activities of others more important than their own. The trouble is, a personality like this is a sure target for deep resentments if overlooked too long.

> *Touching means contact.*

Touching means contact. In the same way that a car with the engine running will not actually move anywhere unless the gears are engaged, many people are stifled in their potential to become more wonderful human beings simply by a lack of enough contact with others. Touch is the conduit through which the current of our communications run most clearly. It is instant access to the soul. But it can be light or lightning, depending on the delivery.

There is more to touching than a hug or kiss goodnight, or an occasional pat on the back for a job well done. And a smack or a shove instead of an expected (and therefore deserved) spanking can be devastating, especially if delivered in error. Once again, this is an area where parents—for better or for worse—have the greatest influence over their children.

Touching is the highest form of acknowledgment and recognition one human being can give to another. It means "you —and you alone—have my full attention and it is my sole desire at this moment to get a response from you." Touching sparks, makes contact, releases the current and tests the temperature of the soul, communicating faster than words... and far deeper. Touching is entering and sharing someone's personal space.

All children long for their parents to enter their personal space. If they resist or are stand-offish in any way, it is only because they have felt rejection at some earlier time. But before you insist how much you love your child and would absolutely die before rejecting them, please realize that the emphasis here is on the feeling more than the rejection. Children do not live in make-believe worlds; their worlds are very real to them. And the feelings that tumble around in those worlds are genuine, whether perceived right, or not.

If Johnny took it as a personal rejection that you chose to go shopping and leave him with the Wicked Witch of the West for a baby-sitter at the precise moment he came down with the flu —then it was. In his eyes it was. And chances are he will never even mention that you out-and-out deserted him in his moment of crisis. If he did, you would set things right, reassure him of his importance to you, and not walk away from the encounter until your relationship was on a firm foundation, again. The trouble is, real life is rarely that neat and tidy.

For the most part, we are not perfect communicators and little incidents like this tend to pile up on top of each other without much notice until there is a fair amount of distortion as to exactly how we feel about each other. Of course they know you would do anything for them, all the way up to shielding them from a bullet if there was a crazed shooter on the loose. But for Pete sake, how often do those things turn up? A kid could grow up by then.

And many do.

Does this mean you should check your insurance policy to see if you and the kids are covered for psychoanalysis to get some of these things that never entered your mind in the first place, sorted out? Not at all. Childhood is full of inappropriate thoughts, inappropriate responses, and enough embarrassing moments to make us look ridiculous if we tried to pursue them all. But we need to cover our bases. Very few hits end up in the outfield when the bases are properly covered. Touching puts a "short stop" to a lot of emotions that could end up on the moon if allowed to go ballistic long enough. A quick response is better than a chase and a scuffle, any day.

Here are a few tips to help you get in the game:

A LIGHT HAND on a child when you are talking to them about something important puts you in their space and automatically triggers their full attention.

A TOUCH OR A SQUEEZE when passing need not have any words connected with it: it means you not only like being in their space, you like them.

HOLD THE BABY. Infants need more touching than the

time it takes to feed and change them. Being held by a parent is such a comfort that it will even override an immediate need for food or dry diapers for a while. So the next time you're stuck in a long line at the market and it's way past junior's time for something, don't just let him howl away in his infant seat. Pick him up.

KEEP YOUR TEENS OFF GUARD with a surprise hug or kiss, no matter what they are wearing. They can't keep those walls around them so thick if you keep breaking through all the time.

DON'T BE PUT OFF by a cool shoulder or an out-and-out effort to escape. It's just a ploy to be chased. Remember, the ones that run need to be caught more than the ones that chase you.

DON'T GIVE UP. A child that consistently resists or seems unresponsive is feeling your contact and making a connection, whether they admit it, or not.

You do not have to be overflowing with emotions of love and kindness in order to reach out and touch your kids. Touching them should be so consistent and responsive that most of the time you do it without even thinking. Automatic. Like catching a ball that's coming toward you, or reaching out for one that's flying by. You'll be making contact every time you do, warding off indifference and resentments that don't stand a chance against the kind of acknowledgment and acceptance that only you can give. Before you know it, they'll be reaching back for you. And when they do...

They'll be touching home.

36

Bad Influences

All parents have to deal with bad influences at some time or another. Whether it's a child who uses bad words in school, drug dealers looking for new clients in the high school scene, or media advertisers who seem to think sex and violence are the only things which appeal to people. There always seems to be somebody or something to watch out for. It is especially prevalent in today's society because—for the first time in history—we allow our enemies to come right into our homes. Through TV and the Internet, both adults and children have access to the world: which is both good and bad.

Good because we've never had so much knowledge at our fingertips, and bad because there's a lot of things out there parents would just as soon have their children stay ignorant about. Like homemade drugs, porno sites, or detailed instructions on how to construct a bomb. Although times (and values) are changing at an alarming rate, most parents still adhere to the popular philosophy of not wanting their children to be so open-minded that all their brains fall out. After all, one of the main goals of a parent is to eventually get grandchildren. Which necessitates our children having to—at the very least—survive their childhood.

The danger of a bad influence lies in its very nature: which according to Webster's definition is "to produce adverse effects on others by intangible or indirect means." Often they don't even look dangerous. One rarely poses an eminent physical or mental threat. Yet all bad influences eventually end up in one of these categories. Sometimes even both. But because of the subtle way they slip into our busy worlds, bad influences—like bad habits—can be at work a long time before any warning signs occur.

When this happens, parent reaction is often aimed at the cause, when in fact, the influence has already taken place and it is the child that needs to be corrected at this point. A parent that cries, "I never want you to see that boy, again!" to a teenage daughter who has just stayed out all night, is not fixing the problem. At this point, he is merely adding fuel to the fire.

There are many methods for dealing with bad influences. Some work better than others, and some, society will not tolerate at all and will therefore take care of for us. Like lawlessness, widespread ignorance, and childhood diseases. The methods of control for these horrors are laws, public education, and mandatory immunization programs. Society exerts its own pressure on parents to maintain these standards.

For example, if you do not immunize your children, they will not be allowed in school, and if you do not provide reasonable and adequate education for your children... they will be taken away from you. This is a far cry from some of our early freedoms but land used to be free, too. We've simply become too crowded over the years. And in addition to the land prices going up, our "right to raise a monster" has been squeezed out by the more popular right of not having to live next to one. Majority rules.

But what happens when society doesn't have enough rules? Before you answer back with, "We have too many rules as it is," let's emphasize that we are not talking about traffic laws or tax violations. We are stepping back to take a bigger look at society as a whole and realize that when the common flea becomes as important as the common man, then society can no longer produce a common good. Because fleas and men (in great numbers) are opposed to each other. They cannot live in harmony and to strive against Nature to achieve this will end not only in frustrating lifestyles, but in the eventual annihilation of one species or the other.

If the law of Nature is "survival of the fittest," then we are wasting our time to hope for a lifestyle without struggles. Success can only lie in shrinking our circles and finding a life-cycle that only interacts with those others that we are compatible with, avoiding the dangerous ones altogether.

A good example of this is to take a close look at an acre of woods. There are many enemies that co-exist within that space. Some get along and some don't. But Nature has designed things in such a way that there are many "societies" living within the same space that have absolutely nothing to do with each other. The day creatures rule the day and the night creatures rule the same space—but at night. Carnivores are not interested in demolishing plant life and insects spend most of their lives recycling debris.

Everyone sticks to their own circle. There are enemies, and there are friends, and rarely do these absolutes change. If by some quirk they do, they do not perpetuate the abnormality to the next generation. Foxes do not show mercy on rabbits one year, and then hunt them down the next. The perfect balance of life in an acre of woods is that everyone knows not only who they are, but who their enemies are, and behaves accordingly. If everyone were after the same thing at the same time in the woodland, there would be utter chaos.

Much of the chaos in our societies, today, has come about because of our propensity to deny many of the impulses of human nature in our pursuit of peace. But it is a false peace we have got for ourselves because of it. That fragile ideal that refuses to recognize the differences in people in favor of our conformity keeps breaking down at every turn. It is not natural for an enemy to lie down with a friend and it never will be. To remove the knowledge of good and evil from our society merely turns us into the prey of serpents all over, again.

If you and your children are out walking in the woods and happen upon a snake sunning itself on a rock, it's all right to say, "That's okay, kids, let's just make a wide circle around him, and if we don't bother him, he won't bother us." But if the same snake is found lurking in some dark corner of your home, the same wisdom does not apply. Because he has already invaded your circle.

It is the nature of a snake to seek out the body warmth of living things at feeding time. He might be peacefully coexisting at the moment, but he will eventually get hungry. This might seem like an extreme example and not many parents would tolerate a situation like this in their home. But if it is true that it is the nature of all predators to feed off the living, then any predator found in your home should be dealt with immediately and evicted. Bad influences are predators. Plain and simple.

> *Bad influences are predators.*

The secret of dealing with bad influences on your children is to:

DEFINE THE LINE BETWEEN GOOD AND BAD. There are a lot of gray areas in today's society. The easiest way to determine if something is a good influence or a bad one is to take a look at what the effects of it are. Bad things cannot produce good outcomes and vice-versa. Is your child afraid of the dark? Then maybe you should cut down on his viewing of scary movies and stories. Be a little more careful of the things you talk about in front of him (like how many people got murdered in your city last week). That doesn't necessarily mean your teenager has to be effected by her younger brother's phobias. But if she is going to watch a more adult movie when it's her turn to choose, she needs to watch it when her little brother isn't around.

MARK YOUR TERRITORY. Decide where your bottom line is and make clear limits for your children. If you don't believe in fighting in your family, make sure you train them in other ways to deal with disagreements. But if you don't agree with fighting unless someone else hits first, they need to know that, too. What are the rules and what are the exceptions? Children need to have these things spelled out for them.

MAKE FREQUENT INSPECTIONS. Bad influences are like cockroaches and other vermin: they make their greatest advances when nobody's watching. Keep an eye on your kids when they think you aren't, talk to them about their day and find out what they really did in school. Spring "Twenty Questions" on some of those friends they seem to be spending most of their time with, to find out if they're really the type of kids you want your own to behave like. Because they will.

GUARD YOUR GATES. Watch out for subtle invasions like parties at someone's house you never heard of, or behavior that" just isn't like" your child, at all. Catch these things early, because if you wait until something goes wrong before you take the initiative to find out why you didn't feel right about it in the first place (first impressions are almost never wrong, by the way) you might have a lot more than the influence to deal with. Your child might already have been won over. Then you'll have worse things than influences to take care of.

GIVE IMMEDIATE CONSEQUENCES FOR VIOLATIONS. You would never say, "A rattlesnake under the table? Hmmm. Remind me to call the exterminators tomorrow." It's the same way with bad influences. If Suzie is spitting at people because her friend Amy does it, this is not the time for a lecture on why we shouldn't do everything someone else does. It's time to correct her for spitting. Period. The lecture can come after if you still think it's necessary. However, most children lose all desire to commit offensive behavior after they have been properly corrected for it.

DON'T AVOID CONFRONTATIONS. It's never a good time for a confrontation, so don't wait around for one. This is one time that old saying, "A stitch in time saves nine," is true. The quicker you deal with things that need to be dealt with, the less of a battle it will be. What's more, your child will start exhibiting better judgment simply because he will be making an effort to avoid confrontations with you. That's Human Nature.

NEVER COMPROMISE. A bad influence is a bad influence. You would never say, "All right, the snake can stay. But the first time it bites one of the kids, it's out of here." If you've let one move in with you, you've already accepted the outcome. People can change: but right and wrong never does. The only time compromise is worthwhile, is in shopping or politics. On the other hand, history proves these things are the first to be laid aside in times of war or famine. Anything that threatens to undermine the quality of your family should never be taken lightly.

If all this sounds pretty extreme—it is. Bad influences are worse than bad behaviors. Behavior can be changed. But bad influences are subtle invaders that feed off your children without their knowing. They do not change. If you do not remove them to accommodate your lifestyle, then you will change to accommodate theirs. That's Human Nature. Your children are the most valuable possession you have. If there are "enemies within" at your house, then it's time to get up and do something about it.

Getting rid of those bad influences is not an impossible thing to do. The truth is, it isn't even hard. In fact, it's easier than changing behavior because it doesn't take half the determination, effort, and consistency to accomplish. That's because a relationship takes precedence over an influence every time. Bad influences are illusive shadowy things that tend to disappear when the wise light of truth is turned on them. The only time they can win over your own strong values is when you ignore them. Abraham Lincoln once said, "Evil flourishes when good men do nothing."

And he was right.

Changing Times

The world is more complicated than it used to be. Having the "world at our fingertips" carries a lot of responsibility because there are a lot of things going on, today, that most of us would prefer not to have on our hands. Especially the things we can't do anything about but have a way of sneaking into our own personal lives until we are forced to deal with them.

Like having a child ask—when you're right in the middle of dinner preparations and still trying to get problems at work off your mind—if a person could survive a nuclear blast by hunkering down in the bathtub, the way they do with tornadoes. Or if washing your hands really gets rid of Covid-19 germs (if you accidentally touched somebody sick) the same way it does for the bathroom kind. Or if maybe you should be considering a move to a new neighborhood, on account of someone said the old uncle living with the family in apartment 104B is really a terrorist.

Even if you are a discriminating parent who not only monitors the TV but knows exactly where your child is throughout the day, there are some influences that happen so fast, there isn't enough time to yell, "Incoming!" Much less, ward them off. And one can get more frustrated at having to answer these kind of questions than what ghost wings look like, if there is such a thing. What's more there is a new debate that parents cringe to encounter, and that is whether everything you hear on the six o'clock news is really true.

Are the monsters in your life taking a back seat to having to check under beds and in closets at bedtime for terrorists or intruders? Children are starting to suspect that a favorite bed toy—including the meanest and greenest of all dinosaurs—is not going to cut it when it comes to the sort of protection one needs against these new threats. Even the adults are scared of these. That's how they talk, anyway, and they never talked like that about monsters and ghost wings.

One cannot—in good conscience—get after a child who digs a six foot hole in the backyard in an endeavor to construct a bomb shelter, when it's a known fact that the neighbors two doors down, have a year's supply of food and ammunition secreted away for the very same reasons. After all, children are only human. Yes, there are things going on in the world over which the individual (no matter how capable and organized) has absolutely no control. Bad things. The kind we would all avoid, if given the choice. The truth is, there always have been.

Every generation has suffered its share of war and hard times, and our times, because of our advances in technology, seem more perilous. Simply because most individuals get a running report of every bad thing that's happening the world over, every evening, around the same time as their supper.

Which is a pretty tall order for us level-headed adults to swallow. No wonder our children are getting concerned. More than a few of us wake up with the startling discovery of some version of the "meanest and greenest of all dinosaurs" next to our pillows: put there on temporary loan from some sympathetic offspring.

So, what's a parent to do?

In allowing ourselves to become too distracted by the things that we can't change, we often miss the opportunities to change the things we can. There are many things parents can do to promote a sense of comfort and well-being in their children. And although they may not have an earth-shaking effect on the state of the world, they can have profound effects on your very own home, every day. A little more light always perfects vision, and even though it might only be in a small corner of a dark place, it might be all a person needs to see where to place the next step. People all down through history have found their way through amazing earth-shaking events that way.

> *A little more light always perfects vision.*

Here are some ways to do that:

ZERO IN ON THE GOOD THINGS. No matter what is going on in the world, the average individual is not omniscient. Most of us can do little more than one thing at a time, and considering there are still only twenty-four hours in a day (even after all these years), that pretty much limits how much we can take in at once. So be picky. Thinking, talking, and participating in good things makes people (especially children) feel good. So, when you have a choice, choose the good things.

AVOID EXPRESSIONS OF FEAR AND UNCERTAINTY AROUND CHILDREN. And don't think because they are busy with something, they aren't listening. Especially when visiting with other adults. Children's ears perk up at the mention of words they are highly concerned about (just like adults), and they have better ears than we do. What's more, they take everything literally. Especially such phrases like, "I just don't know what we'd ever do if..."

BE REASSURING. Take a lesson from the good doctors and nurses who deal day in and day out with human pain and suffering. They have discovered that merely saying, "You're going to be fine," whether they know this to be fact, or not, has an amazing effect on a person's psyche. And history proves that many times, the human psyche will override the facts. People have been known to survive against amazing odds, simply because they believed that they could. And they do.

TALK ABOUT THINGS. If you have to have the evening news every night with dinner, at least make a point of discussing it with your children. Find out how they feel, and what their opinions are about things. Things that never occurred to you might affect them in ways a mere explanation from you could dissolve. Which could help them sleep better at night. Which, in turn, might allow you to do the same.

BE AGE APPROPRIATE. Talking about war with a teenage child is different than talking about it with a preschooler.

A teenager is of an age to need to decide where to stand, while a younger child may be slipping under the bed when the lights are out, and having nightmares about being attacked before morning.

TAKE GOOD ADVICE. If you hear a "parental discretion is advised" warning before certain films or photos are going to be aired on TV, take the network at their word. No amount of explaining can soften the impact of seeing dead women and children piled up in the streets, or angry mobs, in the mind of a child. Images seem to last much longer than words, and take ten times the effort to dispel after they have once gained a foothold into a young mind.

SMILE. A smile is worth a thousand words when it comes to explaining, or reassuring, or trying to convince a child that everything is going to be all right, today. Children have the amazing capacity to lock into a smile in the midst of pain and confusion, or any other outside force, when it comes to focusing in on what really matters in life. If you haven't smiled at your children at least three times in a single day, then make it a habit, so that you never forget to, again.

Times change, but people don't. If you can make it important to emphasize the human limits of every day, your children will follow your lead and do the same. We might not be able to change the course of world events, or even many of the effects those events can have on our individual lives. But we can change the tone of the time we personally have allotted to us, each and every day. And in doing that, we will not only have more peaceful homes to live in, we will be making the most of our choices of how we will spend our time. Don't like the way time has been treating you, lately? Then pick something better to do.

That's the secret of living in changing times.

38

Owning Your Own Home-life

Whoever coined the phrase "time is money" wasn't far wrong. In fact, we have a tendency to spend time in much the same way we spend money. Those who aren't careful where their time goes find that it gets spent anyway. Often on things they wish they hadn't wasted any time on, at all. The thing about time is, while you can give it away — by doing for someone else in order that they may be free to do something else — you can't save it up. Nor can you will any to your heirs after you're gone: unless you do so by the giving method, which is to provide for them in some way so they might better utilize their own time.

Time has no grandchildren.

Each of our lives is an amount of allotted time, broken down in a series of increments that — for the most part — we have very little say in. We get twenty-four hours per day, no more and no less. We get it for the duration of approximately seventy years. A relatively small percentage of us get a few years more, though rarely past a hundred, and an equally small percentage die young, which could happen at any age. Nobody knows.

Down through the years, medical science has done extensive studies that have tried to unlock the reasons for these statistics but they've made little headway. And about the time they decide that good food and exercise extend longevity, they discover some remote village in France where everyone lives to be centurions on a diet rife with cigarettes, chocolate, and wine at every meal. On the whole, however, the general populace has decided not to deal with the subject.

Which brings up another familiar saying that tells us, "Don't waste your time on things you can do nothing about." That could be true, depending on how you look at it. There's a good chance this very same saying was spoken repeatedly in the ears of those who invented the early airplanes and there aren't many of us today who are not grateful that they didn't listen. Then again, the invention of the gasoline engine seems to have done more toward using up our natural resources than all the wars and wildlife exploitation in history. Everything comes down to a matter of choice.

Everything.

And amazingly, choices do make a difference. We might only get twenty-four hours in a day, but—unless you are underage or somebody's slave—what you do with them is pretty much up to you. That wouldn't be a bad arrangement if it weren't for something called consequences, which are also doled out equally to everybody... depending on how you spend your time. No exceptions. No matter where you were born, or who your parents are. Besides that, there are "time robbers."

It doesn't seem fair that one should be able to steal time when we all have the same amount already, and cannot hoard it. Fairness (though equally important, and a very hot topic in some circles), is a different subject altogether. The fact is, that time robbers are not fair, and it's the facts that we are looking at, here.

There are many things that can rob you of your time; from deceptive advertising to an insensitive co-worker that manages repeatedly to detain you after you've mentioned numerous times that your daycare center enforces penalties for parents who pick their children up late. And your own children can also be time robbers on occasion, especially if they have learned that the distractions they cause you usually work to their advantage. But these are extreme cases.

For the most part, time robbers are subtle influences that make you forget what is important and that you are steadily spending your allotted time whether you are wasting it, or not. You forget how the old sayings go, and pretty soon, you are living by the philosophy, "Never do today, what you can put off until tomorrow." You do it out of shear survival, especially when it comes to paying bills or taking care of family emergencies. Your priorities become whatever situation is in front of you that most desperately needs your attention.

It is sad to note that one of the things most quickly set aside in these situations, yet has the most impact on you personally, is your home-life. Everyone, including children, needs a place to rest and rejuvenate apart from the more intense interactions of daily living. It's human nature. It isn't always evident because some of us have more endurance than others, but that, too, is another subject. The fact remains that people who get proper amounts of rest and rejuvenation (which reach optimum levels when linked with peace and order) are statistically more successful than those who don't. And for the record, the definition of peace and order we are referring to, here, is not interchangeable with eight to nine hours of sleep each night, and a live-in maid. Not all of us need—or even want—those things.

We are all wonderfully different in that respect and "one man's ceiling is another man's floor," as the saying goes. One might find rest and rejuvenation on a quiet mountainside that would spell nothing less than horror for someone else who was afraid of heights. One might need a quiet evening alone, while another prefers the company of good friends to relax with. Personalities differ, but the basic need stays the same. And even though we meet these needs in different ways, the same time robbers have a tendency to threaten all.

So, here are some ways to protect time for your own piece of paradise:

DECIDE BEFOREHAND what you will and will not waste your time on. It isn't always possible to make a snap decision but if you've decided against something beforehand, it is easier to recognize the intrusion when it comes and say, no. Simply because you've already decided.

MAKE ROOM FOR THE THINGS YOU LOVE BEST. Don't be one of those who come to the end of life and say, "I wish I had." Is there something you especially love doing but never seem to have enough time for?

Then cut out something you like less.

DON'T TRADE PEACE FOR HAPPINESS. Many parents have a tendency to choose the "path of least resistance" when it comes to pacifying children, or anyone else for that matter. But in the long run, the low quality of satisfaction is a poor trade for true contentment. For everyone concerned. Sort of like that old saying, "when salt has lost its flavor, what good is it?"

PRIORITIZE YOUR SHOULDS. If you find yourself doing too many things for no more reason than you "thought you should," weed out some of those commitments. Amazingly, those organizations and sports leagues, and committee memberships for community affairs, rarely cease operations when members drop out. How many have you gone to where the topic of discussion was who was no longer a member and what the world should do about it?

TENACIOUSLY COVET PERSONAL TIME WITH YOUR CHILDREN. Nothing can replace the benefits that come from one-on-one time with your child: which does not include your voice being the loudest one they hear at soccer practice.

DECLARE A "SAFE ZONE" at some time in some area of your house, where it is against the rules to bring up problems or talk about them. Whether it's at the dinner table or part of the bedtime routine, have some place and segment of your family's day where you only talk and do fun things.

DO SOMETHING YOU CONSIDER WORTHWHILE

every day, whether it is large, or small. This does not mean something that you feel you should think is worthwhile, but something that you really do.

MAKE SOMEONE HAPPY. In little ways, big ways, or anything in between. Not just because it's a great thing to do, but because happiness is like giving: it has a boomerang effect. The more you give it away to others, the more comes back on you. Usually multiplied. Which can have a wonderful influence on your whole outlook in life.

Happiness is like giving: it has a boomerang effect..

Everyone has a home-life, no matter where they live. But your home-life—like your home—is only capable of holding so much. The secret to having a home-life that has more satisfaction and contentment than tension and confusion in it, is to do something different with the time that you spend there. Something that you feel is pleasant and worthwhile, so that you find rest and rejuvenation there instead of a constant drain on yourself. And the way to do that is by taking charge of your time.

Even if it's only in small amounts, you can get wonderful results by doing things "a little at a time." Are you a book lover but you never seem to get enough time to yourself to read? Then decide to take fifteen minutes out of your day, somewhere, even if it's off one end or the other of your sleep schedule. Only fifteen minutes. We waste far more than that just waiting in lines, or at traffic lights. You'll be surprised how refreshing just a little of something you like can be.

Benjamin Franklin once said, "Do you love life? Then do

not squander time, for that is the stuff life is made of." And he was right. You can make changes in your home-life the same way you take on any other big project: by doing it a little at a time. Sort of like house payments.

That's the secret to owning your own home-life.

39

Believe It Or Not

All children believe. Everything. Their values are based on what their parents do—good or bad—because parents are the single most important thing they believe in. That isn't to say, as they grow older things won't change: they will. But for the short duration of their childhood world, children "Believe all things, hope all things, and endure all things." It is a time of amazing promise and possibilities. The only time in life when one is protected by some yet unexplored force field called innocence that is as much a mystery in the new millennium as it has been for centuries.

A mystery and a paradox.

As parents, we take great pleasure—and even solace—in it. Especially in this day and age when so much of what children are bombarded with is outside a parent's control. There is a comforting knowledge that at certain tender ages, even the most explicit of visual impressions goes over young heads. And it's a blessing. At the same time, we tend to exploit some of that believability and innocence, ourselves. In little ways. Mostly because of the absolute enjoyment we get from seeing a full-blown reaction: of joy, awe, or utter amazement cross those little faces we love. A story well told, the promise of a surprise, and the tickle-induced laughter that gives us a laugh ourselves, are among the favorites.

But the all-time best loved of parent and child is Christmas.

We find ourselves making things up just to get the reaction. Like Santa Clause. That legendary saint holds the record for one of the most widely upheld conspiracies the world has ever known. And it has gone on for centuries. Every year, parents band together to create the illusion that this wonderful man never died. They have concocted an amazing tale of life at the North Pole and reindeers that fly. Of one man circling the globe in a single twenty-four hour span to deliver presents to the children of every household.

Children everywhere are prompted to leave snacks out in the kitchen to assist the old gentleman in this difficult task and some parents have even gone so far as to dress up like him in order to seal the proof. Big business and department stores have joined in, paying wages to Santa look-alikes who will listen to the wish lists of children and have pictures taken with young hopefuls. The crowning touch is to turn on the evening news on a Christmas Eve and follow the tracking of Santa across our own continent. Even the youngest of children know that those who deliver the nightly news would never lie to anyone.

Least of all children.

As children grow older, they begin to suspect what is going

on and something truly amazing happens. They do not feel betrayed. Instead, a sort of metamorphosis occurs. They change from being the recipient of this fantasy, to being a promoter of it. Big brothers help weary mothers stay up late and wrap presents for little ones. Big sisters make sure the snacks left out for Santa's yearly quest are the ones their very own father likes best. They take great pleasure in putting secret presents in an unsuspecting loved one's stocking. In short, the dream perpetuates itself and far outlives those who participate in it.

The spirit of Christmas is an amazing thing.

Nearly all parents—no matter what their background or religious affiliation—bend over backward to give their children a happy Christmas. Besides lavishing presents (most of which a child has no actual need for), parents can be found tolerating long lines and horrendous crowds at shopping centers, boring school programs, even more boring relatives, and a deficit in their bank accounts they would never dream of approaching at any other time of year. And they do it cheerfully.

Christmas is a phenomenon.

For one brief season every year, it crosses the boundaries of religion, politics, and morals to benefit everybody. Everywhere. You are not excluded from it if you do or don't participate in the Santa conspiracy. You are not left out if you are Jewish or Muslim. And even if you are a beggar on the street with no money for supper (much less for the party), chances are, someone somewhere will wish you well, smile, or perform some act of kindness toward you on behalf of the spirit of

Christmas. And chances are it will be the same person who has "looked through" you all year long.

Christmas brings out the best in people.

But because of all this extra activity in our daily routines, Christmas can also be a time of added stress and limited time in our already hectic schedules. Many last minute decisions are made that often turn out not to be in the best interest of our children. At the same time, there are always a few "sure things" to fall back on. Like knowing that the best gifts are the ones that last.

Here are a few gift suggestions that can make your Christmas season a better one:

- **KIDS CAN ALWAYS USE A LITTLE MORE PATIENCE.** Remember how limited your children are. If you're tired, they're doubly tired. And if you're a little grouchy because it's late and you haven't even thought about what to have for dinner, yet, they've probably been hungry for the last hour: which effects their whole outlook on life.

- **GIVE THEM THE JOY OF GIVING.** Let them participate in choosing gifts for others. Or let them earn a little extra money for parent gifts, then take some time to shop for them.

- **MAKE TIME FOR A CHOCOLATE STORY.** Whenever your celebration begins (Christmas Eve, Christmas Day, or even twelve days before), take time to read a Christmas story and drink hot chocolate together (or some other holiday drink). Whether it's Dickens, Santa

Clause, or the birth of Jesus, you'll find children remember these stories long after the new toys are lost or broken.

DECLARE A HOLIDAY TRUCE ON THE "EX-WARS." For the duration of the season, make it your purpose not to call names or speak negatives about ex-spouses or in-laws. These kinds of words grieve children in their deepest parts because no matter what infractions have gone on before, they love the whole family. Unconditionally.

DO SOMETHING KIND FOR SOMEONE OUTSIDE YOUR FAMILY. Whether it is buying a gift for an under-privileged family, watching a neighbor's pet while they spend holidays away, or giving to a local charity, let the children learn first-hand that it is "more blessed to give than to receive."

LET YOUR CHILDREN HELP in family dinners, house decoration, gift-wrapping, etc. Even if it takes more time in the long run. Children become by doing. If they are constantly turned away at busy times, they will no longer be interested when you think they are finally "old enough" to help.

> *Children become by doing.*

HELP MAKE "PEACE ON EARTH" by adding your share. Relegate all arguments and disputes to the "Silent Court" in honor of the Christmas season. Stop quarrels in mid-battle by a raised hand and declaration of "Listen to the peace of Christmas..." No fighting and feuding allowed at Christmas. All disagreements must be written down and settled—on paper—by decree of a parent. You will be surprised how easy this is. Not only is peace a tangible thing that you can see and feel at Christmas, a parent has a supernatural respect from children during the holidays... for obvious reasons.

Children are amazingly agreeable and cooperative at Christmas time. As if while sleeping in their beds, some benevolent angel came down and kissed them, parents sometimes wonder what came over the child who is hoping and praying for a certain something under the tree and trying to act worthy of it. And children aren't the only ones. Except for the farthest gone of reprobates, or evil incarnate, everyone participates. And because of this corporate surge of the goodness of humanity in honor of the most admirable man of all history, the "season of Christ" still covers the earth with peace and goodwill for those few brief weeks out of every year.

Christmas truly is a visitation of God in the tributes of men, in honor of the birth of His son. It is the only celebration of its kind. Practiced religiously and traditionally by the majority of everyone on earth... for millennia. At Christmas we give more, love more and do more for others than at any other time of year. And it is the peace, joy and happiness of these times that compels us to carry on with it year after year. Who is to say if —like the Santa conspiracy—at the end of it all, a metamorphosis on the grandest scale might not occur?

And we will all be more like Him.

There are many things to decide on at Christmas. Whether or not to believe in one thing or another often complicates an otherwise simple gift. But one does not need to understand the refraction of light to enjoy a sunset; it's simply beautiful. So is Christmas.

Whether you believe it or not.

"Train up a child in the way he should go: and when he is old, he will not depart from it."

Proverbs 22:6

Helps

Point Game for Younger Children
Point Chart for Older Children
Behavior Contract for Teens

How It Works

For younger children, it works out better to have something more visual than just writing down numbers, or keeping a tally for points on a post-it note on the refrigerator. The example here is something that can be modified to your own needs (such as point values and specific behaviors or chores you are working on).

It can also be simplified for the very young by using a magnet (for playing on the refrigerator) on the larger "rainbow" squares, so that the game won't be so long they lose interest. This way, the game can be completed in a day, or a week, or anywhere in between.

The point wheel allows for "side trips" worth an early reward for those who might choose that option... however the playing piece usually begins in the same place on the "rainbow road" when they return next time.* The point boxes beneath the wheel may be assigned for specific activities, projects, or chores. Older Children might simply want to keep track of their progress by coloring in squares with a marker. Use dice or a spinner from another game for the "Right Now Wheel."

Important Reminder:

Never take points away! A child might be stuck in the same place for a long time until he/she earns more points, but they must never lose what they have already earned. In the same way, those treats or activities you have assigned to the game should not be obtainable in any other way but by participation in the game. The strength of **THE POINT GAME** depends on these two things.

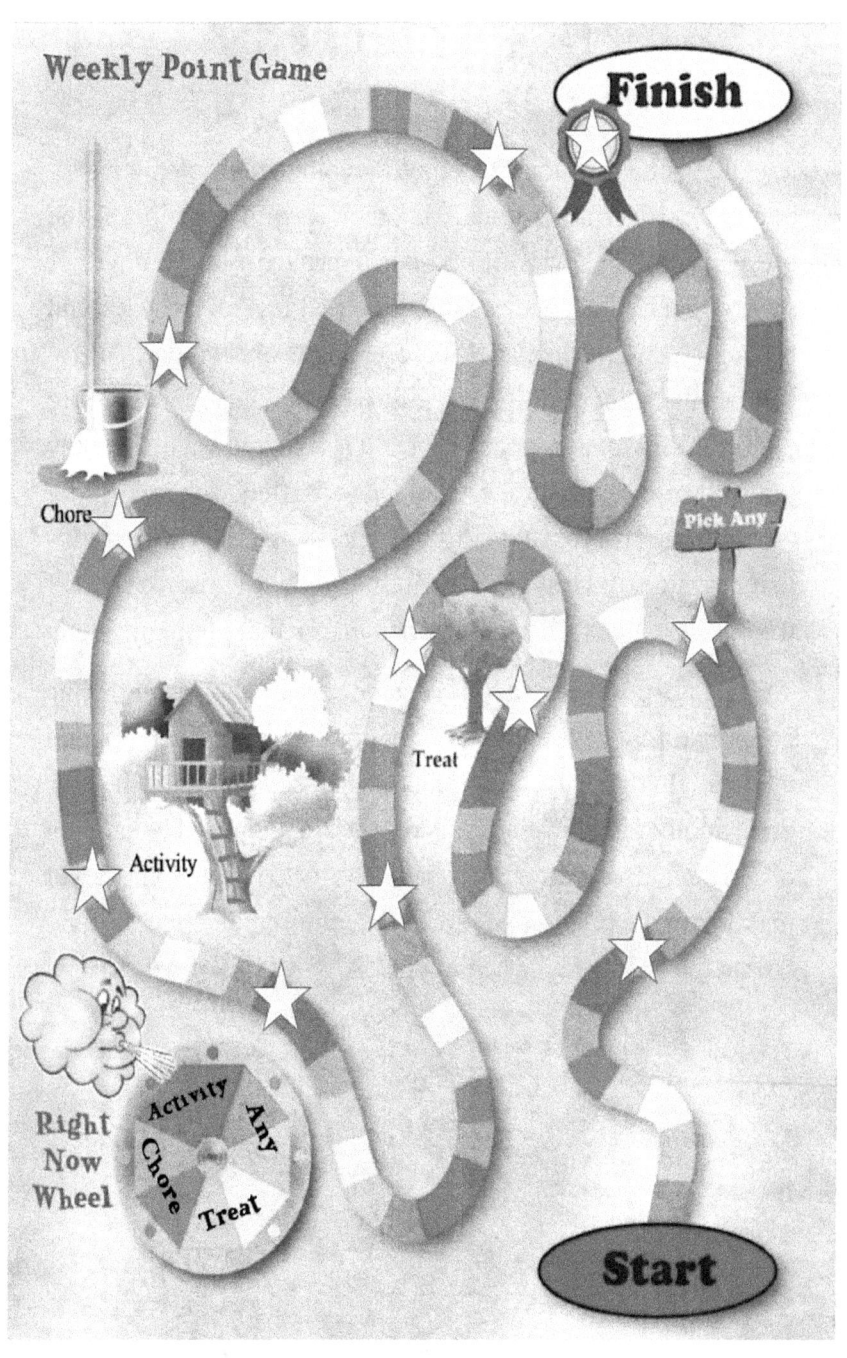

Scan the image so you can put a fresh copy up daily or weekly.
Count squares or stars, depending on the age of your child.

How It Works

Older children tend to enjoy keeping track of their own points, and having parents (or other care givers) initial the boxes when a behavior or chore is approved. The strength of this system lies in – once again – never taking points away, and by deciding on *specific* goals beforehand. For example: Thirty-five points might be the goal for the weekly reward but there are opportunities to make many more. It is also important that they get to choose their own chores and rewards they will be working on each week (point values agreed upon by parent), which adds to their value of the system because they have chosen it for that week. One values what they work hard on: that's human natute.

Use **Bonus Rewards** (decide what these might be beforehand aand write them in) for points that are made beyond the goal. In this way, children become accustomed to moving on to another goal when one is reached, as opposed to backing off on their efforts after the first goal is met. If your child never makes it to the bonus goal, lower the requirements accordingly so that the goals remain achievable. Always set them up to win.

Weekly Point Sheet

Chores & Projects	Mon	Tues	Wed	Thu	Fri	Sat	Sun
Rewards							
Bonus Points							

Weekly Goal_____Bonus Points_____

Total_____

# Contract Agreement For Teens

Teenagers need to be held accountable in ways that are as close to the "real world" as possible. That's why it becomes important that "their word be their bond" in the same way that it is for adults. A written contract such as the sample that follows, works well to remind *both parties* what they have agreed on and signed their name to.

This form of agreement also makes settlements easier and should be handled just as they are in society. Did you agree to these things? Did you perform them? Then you are (or aren't) entitled to the provisions of the agreement. Once again, do not take away privileges already earned, and be reasonable during negotiations beforehand.

Reminder: the more you treat a teen like an adult, the more they will act like one.

AGREEMENT OF SERVICES

This Agreement is to serve as a contract between _____ and _____ for the purpose of exchanging services for privileges and expenses from the period of _____ to _____.

I _____ residing at _____ do hereby agree to perform the following services:

_____
_____
_____
_____
_____

In exchange for the following privileges:

_____
_____
_____
_____
_____

Expenses included for this period: Yes _____ No _____

If yes, these expenses shall include the sum of _____

Agreed upon this day of _____ to last until the date of _____ Or until both parties shall jointly agree and draw up another or modified agreement.

Teen:_____ Parent:_____

About the Author

As a former educator, and co-founder of the Wilderness School Institute, Lilly Maytree has developed curriculum for outdoor activities that incorporate nature studies, wilderness skills, and motivational behavior programs. Many of which were for troubled youth through state agencies.

After years of experience, she has a lot to say about what motivates children, and has implemented many of those unique ideas into books and programs that others can use. She is also an adventurer, who can lay claim to that title for having accompanied her captain husband a thousand miles up the Inside Passage to Alaska aboard their thirty-two foot ketch, *Glory B*, and survived it.

You can get in touch with her by visiting:

LillyMaytree.com

Other books by
Lilly Maytree

Novels:
Gold Trap
The Pandora Box
Neptune's Lady

The Stella Madison Capers:
Home Before Dark
A Thief In The House
Sea Trials
The Pushover Plot
Lost In The Wilderness
The Last Resort
Voyage of the Dreadnaught

For Writers:
Unspoken Rules
Writing Rules!

For Parents:
Behave Yourself!
Teaching children to discipline themselves.

Thank you for purchasing this book sponsored by the Wilderness School Institute. Your support helps us to maintain the website and continue to offer high-quality resources to families everywhere. If you found *The Nature of Children* helpful, please let us know! You can share your opinions and experiences about it over at:

WildernessSchoolInstitute.org

You can also find helpful articles and tips about dealing with children over at:

SummersIslandPress.com

Simply click through to the "For Parents" tab when you get there. You might also enjoy taking a few moments to browse through the many books and activities for children based on the methods we have talked about here.

This Book was published by:

If you enjoyed it, please consider leaving a review in any of the places you like to buy books. To browse other books like this—both fiction and nonfiction—visit:

LightsmithPublishers.com

We appreciate you taking the time to read! We hope you will take advantage of our FREE EBOOKS that are new each month.

About the Authors

Jeff Pepper (author) is President and CEO of Imagin8 Press, and has written dozens of books about Chinese language and culture. Over his thirty-five year career he has founded and led several successful computer software firms, including one that became a publicly traded company. He's authored two software related books and was awarded three U.S. patents.

Dr. Xiao Hui Wang (translator) has an M.S. in Information Science, an M.D. in Medicine, a Ph.D. in Neurobiology and Neuroscience, and 25 years experience in academic and clinical research. She has taught Chinese for over 10 years and has extensive experience in translating Chinese to English and English to Chinese.

www.ingramcontent.com/pod-product-compliance
Lightning Source LLC
Chambersburg PA
CBHW072009110526
44592CB00012B/1251